Curt Walters

Grand

Text: Joni L. Kinsey   Foreword: James E. Babbitt   Picture Editor & Designer: Arnold Skolnick

the Majesty of the Canyon

150 Years in Art

FIRST GLANCE BOOKS, COBB, CALIFORNIA

Published in the United States of America
by First Glance Books, Inc.

Distributed by First Glance Books, Inc.
P. O. Box 960
Cobb, CA 95426
Phone: (707) 928-1994
Fax: (707) 928-1995

This edition was produced by
Chameleon Books, Inc.
31 Smith Road
Chesterfield, MA 01012

ISBN 1-885440-31-6

Printed in Hong Kong

President: Neil Panico
Vice-President: Rodney Grisso
Designer, Picture Editor: Arnold Skolnick
Design Associate: KC Scott
Editorial Assistant: Laura J. MacKay
Copyeditor: Carl Sesar

(page 1, detail)
BRUCE AIKIN
A CHRISTMAS MORN, 1990
ACRYLIC, 24 X 30 IN.
PRIVATE COLLECTION

(page 2–3 detail)
CURT WALTERS
GRAND ELOQUENCE, 1944
OIL ON CANVAS, 30 X 72 IN.
PRIVATE COLLECTION

(Pages 4–5 detail)
EARL CARPENTER
ISIS TEMPLE, N.D.
OIL ON CANVAS, 30 X 40 IN.
PRIVATE COLLECTION

ACKNOWLEDGMENTS

The idea for this book came out of a conversation with Paul Benesek, the curator of the Sante Fe Railroad Collection of Southwestern Art, who had loaned me transparencies of the Grand Canyon for *Paintings of the Southwest*. After informing me of their vast holdings of Grand Canyon paintings, Paul and I considered a book on this subject. As a book of this nature had never been done before, most publishers were reluctant to join me in this majestic venture. As a result, it has taken me four years to bring this project to fruition. Thanks to the vision of Neil Patico and Rodney Grisso of First Glance Books, *The Majesty of the Grand Canyon, 150 Years in Art* has become a reality.

Joni L. Kinsey performed a Herculean feat in undertaking this massive project. This book is testimony to her marvellous abilities. James E. Babbitt provided an invaluable connection to Louis Aiken in addition to writing a fine introduction.

Of course it is to the artists who have tackeled this most difficult subject that I have dedicated this book. I personally want to thank Earl Carpenter, Wilson Hurley, Frank Mason, Daniel Morper, and Ed Mell who opened their studios to me. It was the high point of my research. I also wish to thank all the fine artists who sent transparencies.

The following galleries also provided many of the images necessary to make this book possible. Douglas Sandvall, El Prado Galleries; Trailside Americana Fine Art Galleries; Katherina Rich Perlow Gallery; Diane Small Reid, Dartmouth Street Gallery; D. Roger Howlett, Child's Gallery; Covington Jordan, Zaplin-Lampert Gallery; Nina Baker, Vance-Jordan Gallery; Fischbach Galleries and the Dartmouth Street Gallery. Special thanks to Nedra Matteucci and Cheryl Nace of Fenn Galleries and to Abe Hays of Arizona West Galleries.

I am grateful for the support and cooperation of these fine museums and collections: Darlene Dueck, The Anschutz Collection; Tony Marinella, Museum of Northern Arizona; David Carroll, Utah Museum of Fine Arts; Tiska Blankenship, Jonson Gallery of the University of New Mexico; Kathleen Ryan, Philadelphia Museum of Art; Arthur Olivas, Museum of New Mexico; Lora Stowe, The Dayton Art Institute; Ellen Kutcher, Reynolda House Museum of American Art; Stephanie R. Gaskins, Ipswich Historical Society; Bud Hilker, Harmsen Art Foundation; Courtney DeAngelis, Amon Carter Museum; Charles Rand, National Cowboy Hall of Fame; Todd Sudbrick, U.S. State Department Diplomatic Reception Room; Will Penniston, The Newark Museum; Robert Tucker, Eiteljorg Museum of American Indian and Western Art; Smithsonian Institution; IBM Collections; Santa Fe Museum of Fine Arts; Phoenix Art Museum; Santa Barbara Museum of Art; Fleischer Museum; Springville Museum of Art; Western Cowboy Hall of Fame and Heritage Center; Arizona Historical Society; Cooper Hewitt Museum, and especially the Santa Fe Collection of Southwestern Art, who supplied so many images for this book.

I am indebted to many private collectors with special note to Mrs. Jessie Smith Porter and family; Kathy and Michael Hard; the Winthrop Rockwood family; Mr. and Mrs. A. P. Hays; Phillip Desind; Mike Sholars; Gail Eberlein; Berry and Mary Lou Langford; Mr. and Mrs. Robert Logan; Mr. and Mrs. R. Shuelke and the DeMartine-Freedman Collection

In addition I wish to thank the Grand Canyon National Park; U.S. Department of Interior and Dana Levy of Perpetua Press.

—Arnold Skolnick

TABLE OF CONTENTS

FOREWORD
by James E. Babbitt
11

INTRODUCTION
The beauty of the Grand Canyon, and why it has been
such a popular subject for artists since the 1850s.
13

THE EARLIEST EXPLORERS AND
ARTISTS IN THE GRAND CANYON
A brief history of some of the earliest visitors to the Canyon,
especially the earliest artists, circa 1860.
14

A GIANT LEGACY: THOMAS MORAN AND
JOHN WESLEY POWELL
The nature of the earlier explorations into the Canyon,
and why artists became an important part of expeditions
into the region. Thomas Moran and William Holmes,
the most famous of the Grand Canyon artists, and
their history of involvement in documenting its wonders.
16

THE SANTA FE RAILWAY AND THE
OPENING OF THE GRAND CANYON
The importance of the Santa Fe Railway in popularizing the Canyon
and in supporting its artists. Through a project of trading travel
and room and board for paintings, the Railway managed to accumulate
a collection of the best work done on this subject.
28

VISITORS AND VISIONARIES
A "Who's Who" of Canyon painters, and discusses many of the most
famous artists of the region. Similarities of style as well as differences—
their personal lives and philosophies.
38

PRIVATE EXCURSIONS AND LIVING THE LEGEND
Painters who visited the Canyon through means other than
the Sante Fe Railway. Living in the area of the Canyon, and what
that meant for the development of its artists.
72

MODERNISM AND THE GRAND CANYON
Artists who have chosen to paint the Canyon in a way that differs
from naturalism. Includes futurism, cubism, impressionism,
and many others. Discusses their training, their philosophies,
and their lives in relation to the Canyon.
90

CONTEMPORARY VIEWS
Contemporary views of the Canyon. Another
"Who's Who" of canyon painting, except
it focuses on contemporary painters and their styles. The forces
leading up to these current styles and philosophies.
94

EPILOGUE
The importance of the Canyon to our view of Nature as a whole.
The importance of artists as interpreters and carriers of knowledge.
156

NOTES
157

SELECTED BIBLIOGRAPHY
158

CREDITS OF QUOTES
159

INDEX OF ARTISTS
160

EARL CARPENTER
THE ARTIST'S VIEW, N.D.
OIL ON CANVAS, 18 X 24 IN.
PRIVATE COLLECTION

FOREWORD

by James E. Babbitt

PERHAPS NO OTHER FEATURE on the landscape of the American West has posed more challenges to human endeavor than the Grand Canyon. Prehistoric inhabitants struggled with the rigors of the arid climate and the constant threat of drought to eke out an uncertain living there. Spanish explorers found the canyon to be an almost insurmountable barrier to travel and conquest. As the last blank spot on maps of the West, the Grand Canyon's intricate topography and complex geology were formidable problems for later surveyors and scientists. But most of all, the Grand Canyon has challenged our creative spirit.

Many early writers viewing the Grand Canyon for the first time judged the experience to be beyond the capacity of the human mind to comprehend. "It is indescribable," trumpeted one article, "Grand beyond description." J. C. Martin, editor of the Prescott *Journal Miner*, visited Bass Camp on the canyon's south rim in 1894 and wrote of the hopeless task of adequately describing in words the canyon's sublime scenery:

The man of letters is appalled at its sight, as language fails him to tell of its wonders. The poet courts in vain the muse for harmonic symphony of this king of wonderlands. One's powers of articulation are paralyzed.

But after confessing their inadequacy, writers proceeded to attempt the impossible, filling volumes of prose and verse with descriptions of the canyon's matchless grandeur, thereby creating a vast library of Grand Canyon literature. Irvin Cobb complained:

Nearly everybody, on taking a first look at the Grand Canyon, comes right out and admits its wonders are absolutely indescribable, and then proceeds to write anywhere from two thousand to fifty thousand words giving the full details.

Many also deemed it impossible to capture the Grand Canyon on canvas. Fitz-James MacCarthy, a writer for Denver's *Rocky Mountain News*, visited the canyon in 1898 and declared, "The scene in its stupendous ensemble is too vast for art. You cannot paint a silence, nor a sound, nor an emotion." Prescott newspaperman Martin also wrote of the artist's seemingly impossible task:

The artist stands aghast as he gazes on its cliffs and pinnacles, with a wealth of coloring the secret of whose blending is known only to the infinite. He relapses into despair when he looks down into the depths of its chasms, with its perpendicular walls rising thousands of feet, as his pencil and brush are not trained to reproduce such perspectives. Nothing that the painter can picture can impart to one who has not seen it any idea of its depths and heights, to say nothing of its fantastic forms.

Even painters themselves expressed trepidation at the prospect of trying to paint the Grand Canyon. In 1929, artist William Robinson Leigh spent a month camped on the south rim sketching and painting canyon vistas. Attempting to capture a fleeting sunset, Leigh lamented:

I struggle in mad haste to utilize the moment, but ah! how futile! how hopeless! What a wretched makeshift these paltry pigments! How hopeless to attempt; what inconceivable impudence to dream of imitating anything so ineffable! It challenges man's utmost skill; it mocks and defies his puny efforts to grasp and perpetuate, through art, its inimitable grandeur.

A contemporary of Leigh's, wood block artist Gustave Baumann, echoed these sentiments of creative impotence, considering the Grand Canyon to be an "artist's nightmare." After attempting several sketches, Baumann retreated from the rim, grumbling, "You see a wonderful composition and when you look back, it's gone. See how fast the clouds are moving. This is the reason nobody can paint the canyon."

Fortunately, painters through the years took no more heed of such hyperbole than their literary counterparts, and proceeded with countless thousands of brush strokes to paint a huge body of Grand Canyon landscape art. For almost a century and a half, artists have put on paper and canvas a myriad of interpretations of the canyon's infinite variety of forms, colors, and moods. From F. W. von Egloffstein's gloomy 1857 images of the lower Grand Canyon, to the bright, crisp watercolors painted by Gunnar Widforss in the 1920s and 1930s, to Ed Mell's more abstract panoramas of the present day, artists have produced a bewildering diversity of works depicting the Grand Canyon.

Until now, there has been no serious attempt to assemble and present an overview of the entire Grand Canyon landscape genre. Joni Louise Kinsey and Arnold Skolnick have taken on the formidable task of compiling and interpreting this important body of artistic achievement. The author of a scholarly study of Thomas Moran's early Western landscapes titled *Thomas Moran and the Surveying of the American West*, Kinsey is well-qualified to write about the painters of the Grand Canyon. Her chronological approach enhances our appreciation of the ways in which artistic styles have evolved, and the scope of her presentation adds to our understanding of the long record of artistic output inspired by the "Titan of Chasms." *The Majesty of the Grand Canyon: 150 Years in Art* illuminates both the challenges that the Grand Canyon as a subject has posed for artists and the many imaginative ways in which the creative human spirit has responded.

Flagstaff, Arizona
New Year's Day, 1998

INTRODUCTION

It is old, this Grand Canyon, and yet so new it seems almost to smell of paint—red paint, pink, and scarlet.
—JOAQUIN MILLER, 1901

ANCIENT AND AGELESS, the Grand Canyon is among the most breathtaking of the world's natural wonders. Visited annually by millions of people from all over the world, this vast series of chasms in northern Arizona never fails to awe and inspire with its size, its ever-changing colors and moods, and its startling portrayal of geological forces.

So remarkable is the Grand Canyon that its most frequent description is that it is indescribable—words are not sufficient to convey its grandeur. Only pictures can begin to suggest its extent and variety, and even they are often pale reflections of their subject. But in addition to the site itself, it is to pictures that people have turned again and again to try to comprehend this place, its enormity, and sublimity, and it is to painters that we look for the most faithful and evocative portrayals of the place in all its glory.

Since the Grand Canyon is itself incomparable, art has been the one human endeavor that seems an appropriate metaphor for its creative primordial origins and sculptured appearance. "As one looks out of the mouth of the amphitheater towards the mysterious vista," wrote journalist William Allen White in 1905, "picture after picture forms and passes that might well have been made by some titanic human artist, so admirably does it conform to the rules of art."[1] The canyon speaks to us visually as only great art can. Charles Higgins, an early visitor, reflected, "It flashes instant communication of all that architecture and painting and music for a thousand years have gropingly striven to express. It is the soul of Michelangelo and of Beethoven."[2]

Artists have attempted to capture this natural masterpiece since the 1850s. While few have believed their efforts worthy of the grand original, their work does convey the wonder that inspired it, a sense of that grand, eternal chasm which embodies both the soul of art and the heart of America. Even more than photographs, the paintings bear witness to the sublime and ineffable mystery of the one and only Grand Canyon.

13

WILLIAM ROBINSON LEIGH

GRAND CANYON, 1911

OIL ON CANVAS, 66 X 99 IN.

THE NEWARK MUSEUM

GIFT OF HENRY WALINGTON WACK, 1979

THE EARLIEST EXPLORERS AND ARTISTS IN THE GRAND CANYON

Ours has been the first, and will doubtless be the last party of whites to visit this profitless locality . . . It seems intended by nature that the Colorado, along the greater part of its lonely and majestic way, shall be forever unvisited and undisturbed.

–LIEUTENANT JOSEPH CHRISTMAS IVES, 1861

14

LIEUTENANT J. C. IVES, who arrived at the canyon in 1857, was not only mistaken in his prophecy that the Grand Canyon would forever be an unvisited "profitless locality," he was also incorrect in assuming that his party of whites was the first to visit the region. As early as the 1540s Spanish explorers had wandered near the area in search of the legendary Seven Cities of Cibola. In 1776 a Franciscan missionary, Francisco Garcés, had spent a few months preaching to the native people in the area of Havasu Canyon. And in 1827 the American trapper James Ohio Pattie and a companion claimed to have traveled the length of the Colorado River.[3] Nevertheless, Ives, who was on a U.S. military mission, was the first American government official to explore the floor of the canyon. Just as importantly, among his crew were the first artists, Baron F. W. von Egloffstein (1824–1898) and Heinrich Balduin Möllhausen (1825–1905), both Germans who had been exploring the West with other expeditions for several years.[4] The Ives party moved valiantly up the Colorado River from Fort Yuma in a specially-built steamship in the vain hope that the waterway would prove navigable; then the river and its rocks blocked their way, but the group proceeded overland, viewed the canyon from the rim, then descended again to the river below.

For all his boasting of being the first to witness the remarkable spectacle of the Grand Canyon, Ives obviously had some prior information since he called it the "*famous* [italics added] `Big Cañon.'" "For a long time we paused in wondering delight," he wrote, "surveying this stupendous formation through which the Colorado and its tributaries break their way."[5] But even as he marveled, he wrote the region off as "profitless."

Egloffstein and Möllhausen's published engravings and lithographs of the region were fanciful views tinged with romanticism. Although acclaimed at the time for their faithfulness, their stilted style and lack of color ultimately failed to convey the real character of the unique sights. Original images from which the prints were made, as the recent rediscovery of Möllhausen's paintings from the expedition demonstrates, more effectively captured the appearance of the region, but it was the printed versions that gave Eastern audiences and legislators their first glimpse of the Grand Canyon.[6] In any case, these artists and their images began a long and distinguished era of visually portraying the "titan of chasms," one that continues today.

F. W. VON EGLOFFSTEIN

BLACK CAÑON, C. 1861

LITHOGRAPH

FROM *REPORT UPON THE COLORADO RIVER OF THE WEST*, EXPLORED IN 1857 AND 1858 BY LT. JOSEPH C. IVES. UNDER THE DIRECTION OF THE OFFICE OF EXPLORATIONS AND SURVEYS, A. A. HUMPHREYS, CAPTAIN, TOPOGRAPHICAL ENGINEERS, IN CHARGE. HOUSE EXECUTIVE DOCUMENT 90, 36TH CONGRESS, 1ST SESSION 1861

HEINRICH BALDUIN MÖLLHAUSEN
THE GRAND CANYON OF THE COLORADO, C. 1857
ETCHING
BARKER TEXAS HISTORY CENTER,
UNIVERSITY OF TEXAS, AUSTIN

In the foreground were low table-hills, intersected by numberless ravines; beyond these a lofty line of bluffs marked the edge of an immense cañon; a wide gap was directly ahead, and through it were beheld, to the extreme limit of vision, vast plateaus, towering one above the other thousands of feet in the air, the long horizontal bands broken at intervals by wide and profound abysses, and extending hundreds of miles to the north, till the deep azure blue faded into a light cerulean tint that blended with the dome of the heavens.
—JOSEPH CHRISTMAS IVES, 1861

HEINRICH BALDUIN MÖLLHAUSEN
CAÑON NEAR UPPER CATARACT CREEK, 1858
WATERCOLOR AND GOUACHE ON PAPER
AMON CARTER MUSEUM, FORT WORTH, TEXAS

A GIANT LEGACY: THOMAS MORAN
AND JOHN WESLEY POWELL

One might imagine that this was intended for the library of the gods; and it was.
The shelves are not for books, but form the stony leaves of one great book.
He who would read the language of the universe may dig out letters here and there, and
with them spell the words, and read, in a slow and imperfect way, but still so as
to understand a little, the story of creation.
—JOHN WESLEY POWELL, 1875

EXPLORATIONS OF THE WEST before the Civil War were mostly military, charged with securing and mapping the region, and determining passable routes for trade, immigrants, and railroads. Investigations after 1865 were much more scientific, seeking to understand the areas they visited. In the Grand Canyon, no expedition was more important in this regard than that of John Wesley Powell, an intrepid one-armed explorer/scientist who was the first to descend the entire length of the Grand Canyon by boat in 1869, and for whom today's Lake Powell is named.

Powell's famed river trip was a hair-raising, dangerous adventure in and of itself, but it was also part of his larger efforts, pursued over more than twelve years, to comprehend the complex system of the Colorado River and its tributaries and to determine their future significance for the United

JOHN ("JACK") HILLERS
JOHN COLBURN, THOMAS MORAN, AND PAIUTE BOY, 1873
PHOTOGRAPH
NATIONAL ANTHROPOLOGICAL ARCHIVES,
SMITHSONIAN INSTITUTION

In this historic photograph New York Times reporter John Colburn and painter Thomas Moran pose with a local boy. Colburn and Moran traveled to the West together from New York, and just as news correspondents today report from the field, Colburn sent columns back to his paper throughout their trip, thrilling Eastern audiences with daily commentaries on the wonders of the American West.

States.[7] His grasp of the subject was immense and prophetic; among other things he provided accurate maps and analyses of the geology, correctly characterized the arid nature of the region, and predicted many of the water problems of the twentieth-century Southwest. Powell was also the first to invite an artist of national stature to the Grand Canyon to portray its wonders for all Americans to see.[8] As early as 1871 he had included photographers among his party and an erstwhile artist, Frederick Dellenbaugh (1856–1930), who went on to become an early historian of the area, and he had seen the photographs by William Bell and Timothy O'Sullivan from the Wheeler expedition to the Grand Canyon. But all these worthy efforts paled in comparison to those of Thomas Moran (1837–1926), who joined Powell in the summer of 1873.[9]

(opposite)

JOHN ("JACK") HILLERS
GRAND CAÑON OF THE COLORADO FROM TOROWEAP, 1873
PHOTOGRAPH
U.S. GEOLOGICAL SURVEY PHOTOGRAPHIC LIBRARY, DENVER

Moran and Hillers worked together in the summer of 1873 at the Grand Canyon, with Hillers providing the painter with photographs that he would use back in his Eastern studio and Moran helping to refine the photographer's sense of composition and pictorial sophistication. In this view we see Moran in the scene, perched overlooking the canyon that he was to paint throughout his long career.

JOHN ("JACK") HILLERS
GRAND CAÑON OF THE COLORADO FROM TOROWEAP, 1873
PHOTOGRAPH
U.S. GEOLOGICAL SURVEY PHOTOGRAPHIC LIBRARY, DENVER

When Moran journeyed to Utah from his home in New York to rendezvous with the survey, he had been west only twice, but he was already among the most famous artists of the region. Two years earlier he had had the good fortune to be part of the first official survey of Yellowstone, becoming the first painter to portray that remarkable area. His work during that historic trip helped initiate the first national park when Ferdinand Hayden, the expedition leader, lobbied for the required legislation by exhibiting photographs by William Henry Jackson and watercolors by Thomas Moran to the Congress. The region was soon set aside as a "pleasuring-ground for the benefit and enjoyment of the people," setting the precedent for all national parks afterward, including the Grand Canyon.

Moran then persuaded Congress to purchase his first major painting of Yellowstone, a seven-by-twelve-foot view of its central canyon (1872, National Museum of American Art), which became the first landscape by an American artist to hang in the U.S. Capitol in Washington, D.C.

With these successes, Powell and Moran now envisioned similar possibilities for the Grand Canyon. Working together with the survey photographer, John ("Jack") Hillers (1853–1925), they searched for views to serve as the inspiration for a second major painting. Moran did not disappoint. He produced a Grand Canyon companion to the Yellowstone picture, entitled *The Chasm of the Colorado* (p. 23). Sold to Congress for $10,000, this canvas joined the first in the Capitol.[10] It was to be the first of many paintings

TIMOTHY H. O'SULLIVAN
*LOOKING ACROSS THE
COLORODO RIVER TO MOUTH
OF PARIA CREEK*, 1873
ALBUMAN SILVER PRINT
8 1/8 X 10 7/8 IN.
AMON CARTER MUSEUM
FORT WORTH, TEXAS

18

Moran would create from the great site in Arizona.

In preparation for this achievement Moran spent weeks with Powell and his party at the Grand Canyon. The photographs he and Hillers created together (pp. 16~19) were a valuable resource in the following months as he worked, back in New York, on his large canvas. They also provided the basis for smaller works and his illustrations for *Scribner's Monthly* (pp. 20~21), a popular magazine of the day. *Scribner's* reproduced them in a series of articles Powell himself wrote in 1875 and then shared the beautiful images with the survey leader. Powell republished them in his official government report, which was a masterpiece of exploration narratives.[11]

Powell was a scientist, but also a romantic, an inclination he shared with Moran. He wrote, "Climb the cliffs . . . and look over the plain below and you see vast numbers of buttes scattered about over scores of miles and every butte so regular and beautiful that you can hardly cast aside the belief that they are works of Titanic art . . . But no human hand has placed a block in all those wonderful structures. The rain drops of unreckoned ages have cut them all from the solid rock."[12] Elsewhere he likened the canyon to a great book of the gods, each strata a different volume to be read no less carefully than an important text, and from it could be gleaned the wisdom of the universe.

Of all the paintings of the Grand Canyon created since 1873, perhaps none can rival Moran's first oil, which is the visual embodiment of Powell's theories. It is, like the canyon itself, immense—a massive seven-by-twelve-foot glimpse into time. Darker and more threatening than most of the paintings that followed it, the view is highly detailed and extremely varied in its range of vision and the geological formations it portrays. Moran knew he was presenting the canyon to an audience who had never even imagined such a sight, and he packed his view with every conceivable element, mood, and perspective. At the same time, he captured the very essence of Powell's scientific and visionary insights into the place—the extremes of weather, the emphasis on water as both a creative and a destructive force, and most especially, the almost religious spectacle that places the viewer on the brink of apolcalyptic fury. As early viewers of the work recognized,

> It is awful. The spectator longs for rest, repose, and comfort. The long vista of the distant tableland suggests a sunny place of refuge from all this chaos and tumult, but for the rest there is only an oppressive wildness that weighs down the senses. You perceive that this terror has invaded the sky. Even the clouds do not float; they smite the iron peaks below with thunderous hand; they tear themselves over the sharp edges of the heaven-defying summits, and so pour out their burdens in showers of down-flying javelins.[13]

For Powell and Moran, and for those who today venture beyond the safety of scenic overlooks and comfortable hotels, the Grand Canyon is a wild place of epic proportions. Moran would later write, "Of all places on earth the great canyon of Arizona is the most inspiring in its pictorial possibilities."[14] In his great canvas he not only realized those possibilities, but

19

John ("Jack") Hillers
Grand Cañon of the Colorado from Toroweap, 1873
Photograph
U.S. Geological Survey Photographic Library, Denver

Jack Hillers was not a trained photographer, but had joined the Powell survey of the Colorado River region as a boatman. He became so intrigued by the process that he apprenticed himself to the official photographer, E. O. Beaman, and replaced him when Beaman quit the group early in 1872. It was the beginning of a long and productive career; after the survey Hillers worked as the principal photographer for the U.S. Geological Survey and the Bureau of Ethnology until his retirement in 1900.

THOMAS MORAN
GRAND CAÑON, FROM TO-RO-WEAP, LOOKING EAST, 1873
WOOD ENGRAVING, 5 X 3 1/4 IN.
FROM *SCRIBNER'S MONTHLY* 9 (MARCH 1875): 528
LIBRARY OF THE NATIONAL MUSEUM OF AMERICAN ART,
SMITHSONIAN INSTITUTION

THOMAS MORAN
THE GRAND CAÑON OF THE COLORADO, C. 1874
WOOD ENGRAVING, 7 1/4 X 4 7/8 IN.
FROM *SCRIBNER'S MONTHLY* 9 (MARCH 1875): 524
LIBRARY OF THE NATIONAL MUSEUM OF AMERICAN ART,
SMITHSONIAN INSTITUTION

20

THOMAS MORAN
*THE GRAND CHASAM
OF THE COLORADO*, C. 1874
WOOD ENGRAVING
FROM *SCRIBNER'S MONTHLY*
9 (FEBRUARY 1875): 408
LIBRARY OF THE NATIONAL MUSEUM
OF AMERICAN ART,
SMITHSONIAN INSTITUTION

21

he also set the artistic standard for all that follow.

Lesser-known contemporaries of Thomas Moran who painted the Grand Canyon at about the same time were Samuel Colman (1832–1920) and William Henry Holmes (1846–1933). Colman was a student of the famed Hudson River landscape painter Asher B. Durand, and like his teacher and many of his contemporaries he spent his early career painting in the White Mountains, around Lake George, and in other areas of upper New England. After studying in Paris in the early 1860s, Colman took advantage of the new transcontinental railroad and traveled west in 1870 to paint. He ventured west again in the late 1880s, and among his images from this period is *Solomon's Temple, Colorado* (1888, p. 46), a remarkably evocative view, done in casein on paper, of the interior of the canyon before it became well known to outsiders.[15]

William H. Holmes, who like Moran also traveled with the U.S. Geological Survey to Yellowstone and the Grand Canyon, was as much a sci-

entist as an artist. He increased understanding of the Grand Canyon in the late nineteenth century with a series of panoramic wash drawings produced for Clarence Dutton's *Tertiary History of the Grand Canyon District* (1882), the most thorough geological treatise on the region of its time. Unprecedented in their large scale and exacting detail, Holmes's wash drawings are so accurate that they could serve as topographical maps, but they are at the same time sophisticated artistic achievements in their delicacy of line and sweeping compositions. Holmes also produced paintings of the region, such as the misty *In the Canyon* (c. 1880, p. 24). In later years he went into institutional administration, succeeding John Wesley Powell as the director of the Bureau of American Ethnology, and then directing what later became the National Museum of American Art.[16]

In the work of these men—Moran, Colman, Holmes, and their geologist patrons—the initial work of understanding and appreciating the Grand Canyon was finally underway, setting the stage for the arrival of tourists.

Moran's great picture tells the truth as one sees the truth, gazing upon the scene with the poet's eyes and feeling its frightful grandeur with a poet's soul... no one, save only Moran—certainly no artist of the pen—has found even approximate expression for the unique splendors, the fascination and the awe of this unparalleled scene.

—Fitz-Mac [Fitz-James MacCarthy], 1906

23

Thomas Moran
The Chasm of the Colorado, 1873–74
Oil on canvas, 84 3/8 x 144 3/4 in.
National Museum of American Art, Smithsonian Institution
Courtesy Art Resource, New York
Lent by the U.S. Department of the Interior, Office of the Secretary

This watercolor sketch, made on site with John Wesley Powell in attendance, was one of the studies Moran
used in composing his great canvas, *The Chasm of the Colorado*, the first oil painting of the Grand Canyon.

WILLIAM H. HOLMES

IN THE CANYON, C. 1880

WATERCOLOR ON PAPER, 21 1/2 X 24 IN.

MUSEUM OF NORTHERN ARIZONA,

FLAGSTAFF, ARIZONA

It gave him scenery worthy of his highest powers and reproduction on a scale
and a quality unrivaled even in the lavish government publications, which were
uniformly ahead of most commercial books of the eighteen eighties. This was
Holmes's real triumph as an artistic geologist and a geological artist.

—WALLACE STEGNER, 1953

THOMAS MORAN

FROM POWELL'S PLATEAU, 1873

WATERCOLOR ON PAPER, 7 1/2 X 10 1/2 IN.

COOPER-HEWITT MUSEUM, SMITHSONIAN INSTITUTION

COURTESY ART RESOURCE, NEW YORK

To open the Tertiary History atlas at any of its double-page panoramas is to step to the edge of forty miles of outdoors. I can think of no pictures of the Grand Canyon, literal or idealized, which have so much of the canyon's own precision and stillness.
—WALLACE STEGNER, 1953

27

William H. Holmes
Panorama from Point Sublime in the Kaibab, 1882
Lithograph
From Clarence Dutton,
Tertiary History of the Grand Cañon District, Atlas, 1882
Museum of Northern Arizona, Flagstaff, Arizona
Photograph by Dana Levy

THE SANTA FE RAILWAY AND THE OPENING OF THE GRAND CANYON

I have seen people rave over it; better people struck dumb with it; even strong men who cried over it; but I have never yet seen the man or woman that expected it.
—CHARLES LUMMIS, 1906

UNIDENTIFIED PHOTOGRAPHER
THOMAS MORAN AND DAUGHTERS AT THE GRAND CANYON, C. 1910
MUSEUM OF FINE ARTS, SANTA FE

AFTER THE SUCCESS of his great chasm picture, Thomas Moran painted countless versions of the Grand Canyon for the rest of his long life, visiting nearly every year after 1900 until his death. He became so associated with the place that one of the scenic overlooks along the South Rim was named Moran Point in his honor, and his portrait, coupled with the headline, "Thomas Moran Sketching at the Grand Canyon of Arizona" was used early in the century to advertise the Santa Fe Railway's California Limited Route to the site (p. 29).

Moran's first opportunity to return to the Grand Canyon after his initial trip with Powell in 1873, however, was not until 1892, when the Santa Fe Railway commissioned him to create a painting of the canyon for the company to reproduce as advertising, since the railway was fast approaching the area. It was the beginning of a long and fruitful association between the corporation and artists, and even though Moran only sold the railroad the reproduction rights to the painting, the commission also marked the beginning of an historic collection of Grand Canyon and American Southwest art.

Railroads had already been using art to promote their services for decades. Moran's original trip west to Yellowstone in 1871 had, in fact, been underwritten by the Northern Pacific Railroad, which was planning its route through the Dakotas and Montana.[17] The Santa Fe, more properly known as the Atchison, Topeka, and Santa Fe Railway (SFRR hereafter), also recognized the powerful appeal of pictures as publicity, and it knew that a destination as unique as the Grand Canyon would be a powerful tourist attraction. To this end the company developed an unprecedented and mutually beneficial working relationship with artists, trading paintings for passage and accommodations in the areas it serviced. This arrangement provided artists with buyers for their work and a means of travel to the landscapes that were their subjects, and gave the railway a powerful marketing tool, a growing collection of original art, and a unique corporate image. Having artists at work at the hotels and scenic overlooks at the Grand Canyon was almost as interesting as the natural formations themselves.[18] As the railroad's advertising agent William H. Simpson wrote to an associate in 1915, in a comment that could have been applied to any number of artists:

> *No doubt, you know that Mr. Moran and his daughters visit the Canyon regularly each year. We have purchased several of his paintings, and even if we should not purchase any more, the fact that he goes there steadily is of great advertising value. He constantly talks Grand Canyon when away from there.*[19]

Before the Santa Fe's art program could really begin, however, the railroad had to reach the Grand Canyon and provide reasonable amenities for guests. When Moran returned for the first time in 1892, for example, the SFRR tracks extended only as far as Flagstaff, a long stagecoach ride from the rim. Compared to his first trip on horseback and on foot, however, even that was a luxury, and the painting he produced from the trip, titled simply *The Grand Cañon of the Colorado* (1892, retouched by the artist in 1908, p. 30) was a great success. Reproduced in vivid chromolithography, an early color printing process, it became one of the first "souvenirs" of the Grand Canyon available to a wide audience.

The first trains on the new spur line to the canyon arrived in 1901, and facilities to accommodate guests soon followed. In cooperation with its subsidiary company, the Fred Harvey Corporation, the SFRR built the famous El Tovar Hotel, a structure as luxurious as it was rustic, and it decorated its coaches, train stations, and restaurants with what would become known as the "Santa Fe style." The emphasis was on service and creating a unique image for a special company, and from the outset art was an important part of the appeal.

Besides Fred Harvey, whose restaurants and hotels were known for their efficiency, their excellent food, and their ever-charming waitresses "The Harvey Girls," the real genius behind the Santa Fe's innovative approach to the tourist industry was its advertising agent, William H. Simpson (1858–1933). It was his idea to sponsor artists' visits in return for paintings and to buy works of art outright. Even though the U.S. Transportation Commission in 1911 outlawed the practice of bartering for passage (including the trading of paintings for rail fare), over time the Santa Fe collection grew to more than six hundred works of art, many of which remain with the company today. As one writer noted, "If Will Simpson should ever set about to write a book on 'Artists I have Toted to the Hopi House and Back,' it probably would speedily become recognized as the 'Who's Who' of that profession."[20]

The grand opening of Simpson's program began immediately; thirteen artists, including such notables as Thomas Moran and George Inness Jr., were treated to a three-week excursion in the spring of 1901, complete with a Grand Canyon lecturer who escorted them to the most picturesque sites.[21] The special event would be repeated in later years with different artists, many of whom are represented in this book, and over the years many of the best-known artists of the American Southwest benefited from the Santa Fe's unique patronage and hospitality.[22] Their work forms the core of historic art of the Grand Canyon.

29

Thomas Moran Sketching at

Grand Canyon
of Arizona

A large painting of the Grand Canyon of Arizona, by Thomas Moran, N. A., hangs in the National Capitol at Washington, D. C.

Mr. Moran was the first American artist of note to visit this world's wonder. He still frequently goes there to get new impressions. In his summer home at Easthampton or in his New York City studio, usually may be seen several canyon canvases under way.

Quoting from Chas. F. Lummis, in a recent issue of *Out West* magazine: "He (Moran) has come nearer to doing the Impossible than any other meddler with paint and canvas in the Southwest."

Other eminent artists also have visited the titan of chasms. They all admit it to be "the despair of the painter."

You, too, may view this scenic marvel as a side trip on the luxurious and newly-equipped

California Limited

en route to or from sunshiny California this winter.

Only two days from Chicago, three days from New York, and one day from Los Angeles. A $250,000 hotel, El Tovar, managed by Fred Harvey, will care for you in country-club style. Round-trip side ride from Williams, Ariz., $6.50.

Yosemite also can be reached in winter from Merced, Cal., nearly all the way by rail.

Write for our illustrated booklets: "Titan of Chasms" and "El Tovar."

W. J. Black, Passenger Traffic Manager
A. T. & S. F. Ry. System
111   Railway Exchange, Chicago

THOMAS MORAN
The Grand Cañon of the Colorado, 1892 and 1908
Oil on canvas, 53 x 94 in.
Philadelphia Museum of Art
Gift of Graeme Lorimer

*It is a matter of regret that the United States Goverment has not yet seen
its way clear to convert the most scenic portions of the Grand Canyon into
a National Park. The people ought to own, forever, this glorious inheritance.
There should be no limitations placed upon their perfect enjoyment of it
but such as are necessary for its preservation ... An act should be passed
forever preserving all the natural curiosities, wonders, and scenic marvels,
the game and forests of the region; reserving it from private occupancy, so
that it shall remain in unrestricted freedom for the benefit, pleasure, and
enjoyment of the people; at the same time providing for the granting of
such leases for hotels, railways, stages, and other privileges as are necessary
for the comfort, convenience, and safety of visitors.*
—George Warton James, 1900

30

Gustave Buek, after Thomas Moran
The Grand Cañon of the Colorado, 1892
Chromolithograph
The Santa Fe Collection of
Southwestern Art

32

THOMAS MORAN
ZOROASTER TEMPLE AT SUNSET, 1916
OIL ON CANVAS, 25 X 20 IN.
PHOENIX ART MUSEUM
GIFT OF MR. AND MRS. JOHN KIECKHEFER

THOMAS MORAN
A Glimpse of the Grand Canyon, 1912
OIL ON CANVAS, 30 X 25 IN.
VANCE-JORDAN GALLERY, NEW YORK

THOMAS MORAN
GRAND CANYON (FROM HERMIT RIM ROAD), 1912
OIL ON CANVAS, 30 1/2 X 40 1/2 IN.
SANTA FE RAILWAY COLLECTION OF
SOUTHWESTERN ART

Although the corporate records indicate that the SFRR once owned a number of Grand Canyon paintings by Thomas Moran, today only this one remains in the collection. Like his 1892 painting, it was reproduced in large chromolithographic prints that were made available to tourists as souvenirs and to passengers all along the line. Today these and other prints of this type may still be found in antique stores, flea markets, and auctions—reminders of early twentieth-century corporate advertising and the days when the Grand Canyon was the newest national park.

THOMAS MORAN
A MIRACLE OF NATURE, 1913
OIL ON CANVAS, 20 1/8 X 30 1/8 IN.
COLLECTION OF DAVID H. KOCH
PHOTO COURTESY OF VANCE JORDAN FINE ART, NEW YORK

36

Louis Akin
Grand Kanyon - 1904

The new El Tovar [named for the Spanish explorer who had first visited the Hopi towns, but not the Grand Canyon, in 1540] boasted the most fashionable of accommodations, including a fine big dining room, large fireplaces, a huge lobby decorated with animal heads and Indian pottery, a Music Room, Art Room, Ladies' Lounging Room, Barbershop, Amusement Room, Club Room, Solarium, Grotto, and roof gardens. The building was completely equipped with electric lights powered by a steam generator. Fresh fruits and vegetables were grown in greenhouses, and fresh eggs and milk came from the hotel's own chicken house and herds. All water for the hotel, and for all the operations of Grand Canyon Village, was brought in by railroad tank car from Del Rio, 120 miles away.

—J. DONALD HUGHES, 1967

LOUIS AKIN
EL TOVAR HOTEL, GRAND CANYON, 1904
OIL ON CANVAS, 25 X 50 IN.
ZAPLIN-LAMPERT GALLERY, SANTA FE, NEW MEXICO

VISITORS AND VISIONARIES

It behooves you, oh, of the soulless Kodak and the loquacious guide-book, to come meekly and with bared feet into the presence of this wonder that dwarfs all other wonders of the world, for it is here and not elsewhere that Nature has done her uttermost ...

"FITZ-MAC" [FITZ-JAMES MACCARTHY], 1906

KOLB BROTHERS
THEODORE ROOSEVELT AND JOHN HANCE ON MULEBACK,
BRIGHT ANGEL TRAIL, 1911
PHOTOGRAPH
CLINE LIBRARY, UNIVERSITY OF NORTHERN ARIZONA

ODDLY ENOUGH, the Grand Canyon was not declared an official national park until 1919, over forty years after Yellowstone had become the first to achieve that status. President Theodore Roosevelt had extolled the canyon's virtues on his visit in 1903, and in 1906 the Antiquities Act allowed him, by executive order, to designate it and other large areas of wilderness as national monuments. By the time the canyon was designated an official national park, countless visitors were already flocking to Arizona, seeking their own glimpse of the legendary gorge, enticed not only by the national publicity and the glowing reports of travelers and guidebooks, but also by the paintings produced by artists sponsored by the Santa Fe Railway.[23] Many of these artists have become the "old masters" of the American Southwest, and while the Grand Canyon was not their only subject, it was one of their most important.

William R. Leigh (1866–1955), who became known as the "Sagebrush Rembrandt," first visited the area in 1906 and returned frequently with the support of the SFRR. Like Moran, Leigh was tremendously prolific, and in addition to his hundreds of studies and major paintings, he also wrote eloquently of his experiences in a journal. One passage indicates his rapid production at the canyon: "Three studies to be done in the forenoon, three in the afternoon. An indefinite number of panels to be dashed off of fleeting effects or moods. Others more deliberately painted of characteristic details ... "[24]

At other times Leigh found it hard to paint. "Though I am perched far out on this naked tongue of rock," he wrote on an especially hot day, "where any wandering current of air would surely find me, though I huddle as closely under my sketching umbrella as I can, yet the perspiration trickles from my elbow. And this, let me add, means something in this dry atmosphere.... Some of my colors are melting and only by judicious tilting of the palette are prevented from sliding off."[25] With perceptive comments such as these Leigh's journal offers insightful and poetic descriptions of the canyon, and also some of the most amusing, combining lofty inspirations with down-to-earth observations: "On either side of my ten-foot-wide perch and in front, the eye drops into chasms, two, three and four thousand feet deep," he wrote. "The huge peaks lifting their crests from the depths are not more still than the feather-winged seed pods that bestrew the ground under yonder weed. The rock ... I am tempted to believe has a more fiery hue than usual, as if it were glowing red hot. I think an egg would fry beautifully on it."[26]

From 1908 to 1913 Leigh sold a series of five Grand Canyon paintings to the SFRR, several of which were massively proportioned. Some of these were reproduced on the cover of the line's dining car menus, and became the company's most popular images. While Leigh did paint many other subjects, not only landscapes, he would, like Thomas Moran, become forever associated with his great subject. His format and even his style did not differ significantly from those of his older colleague, but his palette was much lighter. His pastel tones recalled the Impressionists and prevented his work from being as foreboding as Moran's first canyon painting, which had been likened to Dante's *Inferno* and criticized for its lack of beauty.[27]

Inspired by the success of the railroad's growing artists program, in 1910 SFRR agent William Simpson invited six artists, including Moran, the lithographer Gustave Buek, and painters Elliott Daingerfield (1849–1932), Frederick Ballard Williams (1871–1956), Edward Potthast (1857–1927), and DeWitt Parshall (1864–1956) to visit and create paintings for the company to reproduce in their advertising.[28] Such excursions had been held before, but this one was a unique undertaking. "Never before had so large a group of serious artists made such a pilgrimage to the Far West with the avowed intention of studying a given point of their own country," a reporter commented, "and thus will this visit to the Grand Canyon become historical."[29] Nina Spaulding Stevens, assistant director of the Toledo Art Museum who accompanied the group, wrote that their arrival was made even more dramatic because "The artists were led to the rim with their eyes closed, that the vision might burst upon them for the first time in its entirety. All was still with the silence of infinity."[30]

Moran, who had been to the canyon many times before and was over seventy years old, made a few studies, while the younger Edward Potthast, by contrast, "worked indefatigably with brush and pencil and took back numerous interesting sketches."[31] More impressionistic than Moran, Potthast, a European-trained painter from Cincinnati, created vigorous and spontaneous renditions of the Grand Canyon rather than the crisp, detailed compositions favored by his older colleague.[32] Potthast inscribed one "To My Friend W. H. Simpson, 1911" in commemoration of the special event.

Even more unusual is Elliott Daingerfield's work. His idiosyncratic, dreamlike visions are surreal renditions rather than representative portrayals. Dark, brooding images with thickly layered paint, they are comparable to works by such highly mystical artists of the late nineteenth century as Albert Blakelock or Albert Pinkham Ryder. Daingerfield's *The Divine Abyss* (1911, p. 41) and *The Lifting Veil* (1913, p. 40), both still in the collection of the SFRR, contain haunting spectres of rising mist, and even more remarkably, ghostly figures—spirits or allegories of the canyon which suggest a psychic association with the ineffable mysteries of the place. Reflecting the spiritual in most of his work (p. 43) and in many of his writings, Daingerfield's compositions parallel his poetry:

> Strip from the earth her crust
> And see revealed the carven glory of the inner world
> Templed—Domed—silent:—While the Genius of the Canyon broods.
> Nor counts the Ages of Mankind
> A thought amid the lasting calm.[33]

Daingerfield returned to Arizona several more times during his career, gathering inspiration. Known for his remarkably passionate and emotive images, he is one of the most original artists of the Grand Canyon.[34]

Some artists traveled individually to the Grand Canyon under the auspices of the Santa Fe through direct negotiations with Simpson. Many of these painters are best known today through their association with the Taos Society of Artists or similar groups, and their contributions to the art of the canyon are highly significant. Oscar Berninghaus (1875–1952), for example, a founding member of the Taos "school," traveled frequently to the canyon with the support of the SFRR.[35] One of his most important paintings of the region is still in that company's collection, *A Showery Day, Grand Canyon* (1915, p. 46). In this view, unlike the pristine presentations of the natural scenery or the more expressionistic visions of many of his contemporaries,

CARL OSCAR BORG
ON THE RIM, GRAND CANYON, 1932
DRYPOINT ON PAPER (ED 20), 12 7/8 X 12 IN.
SANTA BARBARA MUSEUM OF ART
ANONYMOUS DONOR

ELLIOTT DAINGERFIELD
THE LIFTING VEIL, 1913
OIL ON CANVAS, 32 X 48 IN.
SANTA FE RAILWAY COLLECTION OF
SOUTHWESTERN ART

The oft-repeated phrase, 'Paint from Nature,' is a good one if properly understood: Paint from—in the sense of away—not by her, lest she has her way with you and not you with her. My meaning is made clear by quoting from one of our very distinguished artists— 'what we want is less nature and more art.'
—ELLIOTT DAINGERFIELD, 1911

Berninghaus offered a glimpse of the "new" Grand Canyon, one quite familiar to all who visit it today. Instead of an uninhabited vista into the abyss, he presented a view of a tourist overlook filled with a cluster of enthusiastic visitors who are as much a part of the scene as the natural vista they survey. The canyon would continue to be portrayed as an uninhabited region of rugged wildness but, as Berninghaus recognized, its identity was forever altered when it became a scenic commodity.

Many other painters of the Taos School were included in the SFRR's art program. Ernest Blumenschein (1874–1960) began creating works for the company in 1911. He was one of the first European-American artists to settle in Taos, and also a principal founder of the Society of Artists there. Blumenschein's long and fruitful life parallels the Southwest's development; his painting *Canyon Red and Black* (1934, p. 52) is a striking example of the work from the second half of his career.[36] Other members of the Taos group, Walter Ufer (1876–1936) and Eanger Irving Couse (1866–1936), are best known for narrative images and other landscapes, but their art of the Grand Canyon is just as compelling. From Couse's interest in Native Americans to Ufer's sun-filled vistas, their images of the canyon embody the full range of their stylistic inclinations.

Similiar to Couse's *At the Canyon's Rim* is Warren E. Rollins's *Indians at the Grand Canyon* (1908, p. 62). The Native Americans who stand at the rim overlooking the massive gorge not only recall the generations of inhabitants who preceded European-Americans in the Colorado River region, but also demonstrate how the artists of the twentieth century and the Santa Fe Railway capitalized on their uniqueness and their appeal in the art of the Southwest. The landscape of the Grand Canyon is made even more distinctive by the Native American presence, lending it an aura of both ancient mystery and contemporary familiarity.

Rollins, who lived in Santa Fe, New Mexico, rather than in Taos, became one of the early masters of that well-known art community. His colleagues there, such as Gerald Cassidy (1879–1934) or Louis Hovey Sharp (1875–1946), also worked at the Grand Canyon early in the century with the help of the SFRR. For the most part, they used an Impressionist palette, but each responded to his own unique vision, adding to the growing imagery of the canyon and of the Southwest as a distinctive region. Sharp's paintings— such as his *Inner Gorge, Grand Canyon* (p. 58), in which we see an early sightseeing excursion—often include small figures. Cassidy's view, *Grand Canyon* (p. 57), by contrast, is a pastel study of light and tone, almost a Southwestern version of Monet's late series of haystacks which are so high key in their tonality as to be virtually abstract.

Los Angeles painters John Bond Francisco (1863–1931) and Carl Oscar Borg (1879–1947) also traveled to the canyon with the SFRR's help. Bond had risen to prominence in California by the 1880s on the strength of his talents as a visual artist and as a violinist. Trained in Munich and Paris, his work evolved into an impressionistic style by 1906 when he produced several views of the Grand Canyon which the SFRR reproduced on its brochures and advertisements.

The Swedish-born Borg became a leading figure in the cultural life of Los Angeles after the turn of the century, so much so that he attracted the attention and patronage of Phoebe Apperson Hearst (mother of the famed newspaper magnate William Randolph Hearst).[37] Although he reveled in the support of such clients, Borg found a more reliable livelihood by painting for the Santa Fe Railway, the Hollywood movie industry, and such tourist-oriented companies as the Automobile Club of Southern California. Such work was necessary, especially during the Great Depression, but Borg disliked commercial commissions and wrote after one such project "thank goodness it is over with. It has been a tedious and thankless job and I am free once more."[38]

Borg found real freedom at the Grand Canyon and in other open spaces of the West. His view *Hermit Camp, Grand Canyon* (1917, p. 54), from the collection of the Santa Fe Railway, is unusual in its focus on the tiny cluster of cabins that formed this tourist outpost, and its cool palette differs noticeably from the more common earth tones of most canyon paintings. But more often Borg's work was traditional, either depicting pristine natural views or scenes with tiny figures moving through the buttes and rocks, as in

This must be the place of departed souls, for here all things endure.
—HARRIET MONROE, 1906

ELLIOTT DAINGERFIELD
THE DIVINE ABYSS, 1911
OIL ON CANVAS, 30 X 20 IN.
SANTA FE RAILWAY COLLECTION
OF SOUTHWESTERN ART

41

The Hush of Evening (c. 1925, p. 60). Borg was also versatile; his work ranged from strongly rendered pen and ink drawings and intimate scenes in nature to sweeping vistas and vividly colored views. Like other Southwestern artists of the time, he drew on a close identification with the land and its people; when he died he asked that his ashes be scattered from the rim of the Grand Canyon.

Borg's *Hermit Camp* compares closely to John Miller White's impressionistic painting of the same name (p. 55).[39] The towering formation of Pima Point in this suggestive view is even more dominant over the tiny camp. Nestled on the rise known as the Tondo Platform, Hermit Camp had become a Harvey Company outpost in 1912, the destination of trail rides and an overnight haven for adventuresome tourists. Originally constructed as the terminus of Hermit Rim Road, which was an alternative to the tolls on the more accessible Bright Angel Trail, Hermit Camp hosted visitors there until 1930, when the New South Kaibab Trail and Phantom Ranch were built.[40]

Another California commercial artist and contemporary of Borg's, Hanson Duvall Putuff (1875–1972) visited the Grand Canyon in 1926 through the SFRR art program. His strongly modeled views (p. 59) often have small foreground figures that "stand in" for the viewer overlooking the gorges, while the forms towering in the distance are like backdrops, reminiscent of work he produced in his early career as a diorama painter for the Los Angeles Museum of Natural History.

Many artists of Putuff's generation earned part of their living as mural painters. Edgar Alwin Payne (1883–1947), for example, worked steadily in this form throughout the 'teens, both in Chicago and in Laguna Beach, California where he helped found that community's Art Association. In 1916 the SFRR first asked him to produce views of the Grand Canyon for them. He traveled the Southwest frequently after that, changing from an impressionistic style to a bolder, more cubistic one.[41]

Oscar B. Jacobson (b. 1882) also worked impressionistically in his efforts for the Santa Fe Railway. Highlighting the effects of contrasting colors through brushwork not unlike that of Vincent van Gogh, Jacobson emphasized the canyon's dramatic hues, lighting, and epic forms. Jacobson later went on to direct the art program at the University of Oklahoma and to launch a school of Native American art in that state through a group known as the Kiowa Five that he encouraged and sponsored.[42]

Not all Grand Canyon views, even in the early days, were made during the summer tourist season. George Gardner Symons (1862–1930), for example, specialized in snow scenes, as his *Morning Shadows, Grand Canyon* (p. 64) attests. A European-trained painter from Chicago, Symons preceded Edgar Payne at the artists colony in Laguna Beach, California, and he contributed

to the SFRR art program in 1914 with his views of the varied seasons and moods in northern Arizona. In his interest in winter scenes he demonstrated his connection with such Pennsylvania Impressionists of the early twentieth century as Walter Schofield, who was known for such scenes and with whom he had worked in England.[43]

The new accessibility to the Grand Canyon offered by the Santa Fe Railway allowed women as well as men a convenient way to visit the region, and so several women artists traveled there through the patronage of the SFRR. Mabel Frazer (1887–1982), for example, an early art professor at the University of Utah, traveled there in 1928. From the experience, her *North Rim* (p. 68), using an intense palette that builds upon the Grand Canyon's own distinctive coloration, accentuates its brilliant light and suggestive moods. Her emphasis on deep blues and soft greens, contrasted with their complements of yellows and oranges, demonstrates her willingness to experiment and constitutes an important contribution to the artistic development in her home region. "It was often the women artists who led the way in the very slow development of modernism in conservative Utah," one scholar has written, ". . . and so they were used and then left pretty much alone to experiment more than their male counterparts."[44]

Among the most interesting women painters of the Grand Canyon is Edith Hamlin (1902–1992). Hamlin had studied at the California School of Fine Arts in the 1920s, lived in New York and San Francisco, and vacationed in New Mexico and Arizona. Through the federally sponsored WPA art program, she painted murals in California in the 1930s, where she renewed her friendship with the much older painter Maynard Dixon (1875–1946) whom she had first met in 1920. They married in 1937, settled in Tucson two years later, and made regular trips to the Grand Canyon, which was near their summer home.[45] During that time, Hamlin received a commission from the SFRR to paint two major murals in the company's Chicago ticket office. Her *Canyon of Flame and Storm* (1940, p. 70) was an outgrowth of this commission and is an excellent example of her work; a *tour de force* of coloristic effects. Its fiery reds and oranges reveal the canyon at its most intense and the scene glows under her touch.

Bostonian Marion Boyd Allen (1862–1941) also traveled widely throughout the United States and Canada in the 1920s and 1930s, including to the Grand Canyon. She had not even attempted art until the age of forty, when she enrolled at the Boston Museum of Fine Arts School, but she quickly won critical approval and exhibited energetically. Her simple yet powerful view, *Cedar Mountain in Shadow—Grand Canyon* (1933, p. 71), was probably among the works she exhibited at the Boston Art Club in 1936 when the *Boston Globe* pronounced the show "the most astonishing exhibition of the season."

43

ELLIOTT DAINGERFIELD
The Spirit of the Storm, c. 1912
Oil on canvas, 36 x 48 3/8 in.
Reynolda House, Museum of American Art
Winston-Salem, North Carolina

While he uses sufficient of the Canyon form to make us sure of what we see, he tells us, for instance, of the silence of the Canyon. That he manifests and expresses by the use of a great figure. . . . Or again, he will tell you of the vast age and somnolence of this great freak of nature, and we find carved into the rocks titan figures of vast proportions sleeping in the midst of the silence; or if he calls a storm into being, he symbolizes the Storm Spirit.
—ELLIOTT DAINGERFIELD, N.D.

44

EDWARD HENRY POTTHAST
GRAND CANYON SCENE, 1911
OIL ON CANVAS, 15 X 19 1/2 IN.
MUSEUM OF NORTHERN ARIZONA, FLAGSTAFF, ARIZONA

EDWARD HENRY POTTHAST
THE GRAND CANYON, 1910
OIL ON CANVAS, 30 X 40 IN.
THE ANSCHUTZ COLLECTION, DENVER

As I peered over the far edge of all familiar things, and I saw the storm clouds roll and flash in the gulf below, the rainbows tangled in the hanging woods, the sunlight turning the mist to drifting smoke and the vast shadowy walls into ruined empires, I kept muttering to myself that it had been set there as a sign. I felt wonder and awe, but at the heart of them a deep rich happiness.

—J. B. PRIESTLY, 1937

Oscar Berninghaus
A Showery Day, Grand Canyon, 1915
Oil on canvas, 30 x 40 in.
Santa Fe Railway Collection of
Southwestern Art

Samuel Colman
Solomon's Temple, Colorado, 1888
Casein on paper, 10 1/2 x 26 in.
Courtesy of Vance-Jordan Gallery, New York

48

WILLIAM ROBINSON LEIGH
GRAND CANYON, 1911
OIL ON CANVAS, 37 X 61 IN.
SANTA FE RAILWAY COLLECTION OF
SOUTHWESTERN ART

WILLIAM ROBINSON LEIGH
GRAND CANYON, N.D.
OIL ON CANVAS, 30 X 60 IN.
SANTA FE RAILWAY COLLECTION OF
SOUTHWESTERN ART

. . . a visitor to the chasm or to any other famous scene must necessarily come there (for so is the human mind constituted) with a picture of it created by his own imagination. He reaches the spot, the conjured picture vanishes in an instant, and the place of it must be filled anew. Surely no imagination can construct out of its own material any picture having the remotest resemblance to the Grand Cañon.

—CLARENCE DUTTON, 1882

Oscar Berninghaus
Grand Canyon Stream, n.d.
Oil on board, 13 x 17 in.
Courtesy Nedra Matteucci's Fenn Galleries
Santa Fe, New Mexico

Edward Henry Potthast
Bright Angel Canyon, Grand Canyon, n.d.
Oil on canvas, 31 x 41 in.
Santa Fe Railway Collection
of Southwestern Art

53

ERNEST L. BLUMENSCHEIN
CANYON, RED AND BLACK, 1934
OIL ON CANVAS, 40 X 50 IN.
PHOTOGRAPH © DAYTON ART INSTITUTE,
GIFT OF MR. JOHN G. LOWE (1935.14)

The River is only one of the many agencies of the great law of change—change whereby the world is renewed and kept virile and living. It is an elemental force and perhaps too remote from human endeavor to be rightly comprehended. We test it by intellectual or economic standards and find it a great unconformity, an anomaly, an extravagance—something incomprehensible. We try to utilize it but it defies us. We think to make application of it in art and literature, but it does not respond.

—JOHN C. VAN DYKE, 1920

HANSON DUVALL PUTHUFF
GRAND CANYON, N.D.
OIL ON CANVAS, 72 1/4 X 96 1/3 IN.
FLEISCHER MUSEUM,
SCOTTSDALE, ARIZONA

CARL OSCAR BORG
HERMIT CAMP, GRAND CANYON, 1917
OIL ON CANVAS, 40 X 30 IN.
SANTA FE RAILWAY COLLECTION OF
SOUTHWESTERN ART

*[Hermit Camp] was built in 1911 by the Santa Fe for
tourist use exclusively and to avoid paying the toll on the
privately owned Bright Angel. There was an overnight resort
at Hermit Camp which has been abandoned now that the
more sumptuous Phantom Ranch is in operation.... The
name Hermit was given to it in honor of Louie Boucher
who was the original hermit of Grand Canyon and who
looked and acted the part.*
—EDWIN CORLE, 1946

54

JOHN MILLER WHITE
HERMIT CAMP, GRAND CANYON, 1915
OIL ON CANVAS, 32 X 42 IN.
SANTA FE RAILWAY COLLECTION OF
SOUTHWESTERN ART

WALTER UFER

GRAND CANYON FROM EL TOVAR, 1905

OIL ON CANVAS, 24 X 30 IN.

SANTA FE RAILWAY COLLECTION OF

SOUTHWESTERN ART

The traveler on the brink looks from afar and is overwhelmed with the
sublimity of massive forms; the traveler among the gorges stands in the presence
of awful mysteries—profound, solemn and gloomy.

—JOHN WESLEY POWELL, 1906

GERALD CASSIDY

GRAND CANYON, N.D.

OIL ON CANVAS, 14 X 18 IN.

COURTESY NEDRA MATTEUCCI'S FENN GALLERIES,

SANTA FE, NEW MEXICO

58

LOUIS HOVEY SHARP
INNER GORGE, GRAND CANYON, N.D.
OIL ON CANVAS, 36 X 48 IN.
SANTA FE RAILWAY COLLECTION OF
SOUTHWESTERN ART

HANSON DUVALL PUTHUFF
GRAND CANYON FROM MAICORA POINT, N.D.
OIL ON CANVAS, 60 1/2 X 72 1/2 IN.
FLEISCHER MUSEUM, SCOTTSDALE, ARIZONA

60

...we have here with us today the dean of America's landscape painters, Mr. Thomas Moran, and Mr. Moran stated to me in the hearing of a dozen others that he considered you preeminently the highest rate of any artist in America today. Mr. Moran is not a man who slops over in praise of other artists' work—in fact quite the reverse. Mr. Moran stated that we did not have a painting of the Grand Canyon in the hotel today that comes anywhere near showing the artistic skill displayed in the picture you sent me.
—CHARLES A. BRANT, 1916

We are in Arizona! The desert! My desert! The land with the red earth, the sunburnt vastness with its blue mountains....This is a big, lonely country....Here one is much nearer the creator of all....There is something ethereal about it—sometimes it is blue, sometimes red, yellow or pure gold. But there is also the most impenetrable darkness; it is more than black and it seems as endless as the night sky.
—CARL OSCAR BORG, 1937

CARL OSCAR BORG
THE HUSH OF EVENING, C. 1925
OIL ON CANVAS, 34 X 30 IN.
COLLECTION OF MR. AND MRS. A. P. HAYS,
PARADISE VALLEY

One day, a five-year-old girl walked up to the rim of the *Grand Canyon* at El Tovar, gazed speechless at the sea of silent colors, then turned to her father with wonder in her eyes. "Daddy," she asked, "what happened?"

—MINER R. TILLOTSON AND FRANK J. TAYLOR, 1929

Some eve'n hour, in silent dusk,
I see the garden of my dreams.
And while the image that I've
Made to live stands inside,
Smiling and serene, I shall go in
And take my own and fold the whole
With the embrace of my soul.

—POEM BY CARL OSCAR BORG, 1986

61

OSCAR B. JACOBSON
GRAND CANYON, ACQUIRED 1916
OIL ON CANVAS, 42 X 32 IN.
SANTA FE RAILWAY COLLECTION OF
SOUTHWESTERN ART

62

WARREN E. ROLLINS
INDIANS AT THE GRAND CANYON, 1908
OIL ON CANVAS, 46 5/8 X 67 1/2 IN.
STATE DEPARTMENT, WASHINGTON, D.C.

EANGER IRVING COUSE
AT THE CANYON'S RIM, 1918
OIL ON CANVAS, 24 X 29 IN.
SANTA FE RAILWAY COLLECTION OF SOUTHWESTERN ART

63

The Navajo Indians, who have lived for many generations on the Painted Desert adjoining the Canyon to the east, told of a great flood, paralleling the biblical account. During this period of protracted rainfall, the Navajos say, the sea rose to great heights, and finally found an outlet for itself by cutting a gigantic chasm into the very depths of the earth.
—MINER R. TILLOTSON AND FRANK J. TAYLOR, 1929

65

JOHN BOND FRANCISCO
GRAND CANYON, N.D.
OIL ON CANVAS, 34 X 46 IN.
FLEISCHER MUSEUM
SCOTTSDALE, ARIZONA

*Not only the color undergoes change from dawn to dusk but the forms shift,
appearing and seemingly disappearing with varying lights ... No doubt the Spaniards
attributed the appearance to things supernatural, but it was then, as now, merely an
illusion brought about by light. The planes of landscape are greatly flattened and often
disappear under direct overhead light. Perspective is wrecked, distance is telescoped, lines are
blurred, surfaces are deadened into mere tints, objects at a distance are confused with
objects near at hand, and often a blue haze of atmosphere perhaps blots them out entirely.*
—JOHN VAN DYKE, 1920

GEORGE GARDNER SYMONS
GRAND CANYON, 1914
OIL ON CANVAS, 47 X 70 1/2 IN.
FLEISCHER MUSEUM,
SCOTTSDALE, ARIZONA

The Grand Canyon is not a solitude. It is a living, moving, pulsating being, ever changing in form and color, pinnacles and towers springing into being out of unseen depths. From dark shades of brown and black, scarlet flames suddenly flash out and then die away into stretches of orange and purples. How can such a shifting, animated glory be called "a thing?" It is a being, and among its upper battlements, its temples, its amphitheathers, its cathedral spires, its arches and its domes, and in the deeper recesses of its inner gorge its spirit, its soul, the very spirit of the living God himself lives and moves and has its being.
—RICHARD BREWSTER STANTON, 1906

GEORGE GARDNER SYMONS
GRAND CANYON, 1914
OIL ON CANVAS, 47 X 70 1/2 IN.
FLEISCHER MUSEUM, SCOTTSDALE, ARIZONA

Wherever we reach the Grand Cañon in the Kaibab it bursts upon the vision in a moment. Seldom is any warning given that we are near the brink....Reaching the extreme verge the packs are cast off, and sitting upon the edge we contemplate the most sublime and awe-inspiring spectacle in the world.
—CLARENCE DUTTON, 1882

68

MABEL FRAZER
NORTH RIM, 1928
OIL ON CANVAS, 33 X 57 3/4 IN.
SPRINGVILLE MUSEUM OF ART, UTAH

This party all went to the river without a guide. They rated it very grand, and all that has been claimed. However, if future parties of camping ladies intend going down, I would advise them to employ the guide, and go prepared for roughing it. The ladies should wear very short wide skirts, and have Hance's burrows to help them up from the cabin.

—Mrs. Lillian B. Upson, 1892

Edith Hamlin

Canyon of Flame and Storm, 1940

Oil on canvas, 40 x 48 in.

Private collection

Marion Boyd Allen

Cedar Mountain in Shadow, 1933

Oil on canvas, 20 x 24 in.

Courtesy Childs Gallery, Boston

PRIVATE EXCURSIONS AND LIVING THE LEGEND

Once an artist who loved the wilderness brought his bride to the head of Bright Angel Trail...he held her very tightly as she looked out across the miles and miles of tumult of form and riot of color that seemed to swirl thousands of feet below her and around her. As from the clouds she looked down into an illimitable, red-tinged, ash-colored hell, abandoned and turned to stone aeons and aeons ago, she stared at the awful thing for a long minute, and then, as the tears of inexplicable emotion dimmed her eyes, she turned and cried vehemently at her artist husband: "If you ever try to paint that, I'll leave you!"

—William Allen White, 1905

Not all artists of the Grand Canyon visited it through Santa Fe sponsorship. As early as 1885, for example, Albert Tissandier (1839–1906), a French illustrator and architect, traveled throughout the United States as a foreign correspondent for the journal *La Nature*. Included among his destinations was the Grand Canyon and Yellowstone National Park. Trained at the prestigious École des Beaux Arts in Paris, Tissandier was an accomplished draughtsman and during his ambitious journey, undertaken before the West was thoroughly developed, he produced over three hundred drawings, many of which he reproduced in a book, *Six Mois aux États Unis* (1886, p. 73).[46] Tissandier's original work, a remarkable corpus of images now in the collection of the Utah Museum of Fine Arts, exhibits the fine detail emphasized by the École and a corresponding attention to the subtlety of the Grand Canyon and its formations.[47]

ALBERT TISSANDIER
MARBLE CANYON NEAR PAGUMP VALLEY, 1885
GRAPHITE ON PAPER, 13 7/8 X 10 1/2 IN.
UTAH MUSEUM OF FINE ARTS, UNIVERSITY OF UTAH
FRIENDS OF THE ART MUSEUM COLLECTION (1978.242)

ALBERT TISSANDIER
GRAND CANYON OF THE COLORADO, 1885
INK ON PAPER, 13 1/8 X 10 IN.
UTAH MUSEUM OF FINE ARTS, UNIVERSITY OF UTAH
FRIENDS OF THE ART MUSEUM COLLECTION (1978.231)

HIROSHI YOSHIDA
GRAND CANYON, 1914
WOODBLOCK PRINT
GRAND CANYON NATIONAL PARK
COURTESY OF PERPETUA PRESS
PHOTOGRAPH BY DANA LEVY

Other foreigners have come too, of course, just as they do today, to view the famous spectacle. In 1914, Japanese printmaker Hiroshi Yoshida visited the canyon and produced a series of evocative woodblock prints which are now in the Grand Canyon National Park collection. Like the later, even more dramatic woodcut views by Howard Cook (1901–1980), in Yoshida's graphic images the power of the canyon's geometry is emphasized over its coloristic effects.

For those who wished a longer encounter with the Grand Canyon, simply making a visit, even an extended one, seemed insufficient. With the amenities provided by the Santa Fe Railway and the Harvey Company in the early years of this century, it became possible not only to visit the area but, for a fortunate few, to *live* there. The first artist to make the place his home was Louis Akin (1868–1913), a Portland, Oregonian who had been working in

New York until SFRR agent Simpson invited him to Arizona to paint the Hopi people in 1903. Akin not only accepted the invitation but stayed eighteen months among the Hopi, becoming an accepted member of their community and forming affinities with the culture that would remain with him the rest of his life.

After completing a sizable number of paintings, Akin returned to New York in 1904 to exhibit his work. While there he suggested to his friends that they might begin an artists colony in the Southwest, and although his hopes did not materialize, his work was warmly received. One reviewer wrote, "We call his pictures of scenes in the Grand Canyon 'landscapes,' but it would be perhaps more accurate to call them visions. . . . Painting them with a keen eye for substance, but more especially with a feeling for the subtle atmospheric phenomena enveloping his scenes, Mr. Akin has set upon the canvas

74

HOWARD COOK
GRAND CANYON, 1927
WOODCUT ON PAPER, 12 X 15 IN.
ARIZONA WEST GALLERIES,
SCOTTSDALE, ARIZONA

HOWARD COOK
COLORADO RIVER, 1927
WOODCUT ON PAPER,
14 1/16 X 8 1/8 IN.
ARIZONA WEST GALLERIES,
SCOTTSDALE, ARIZONA

chromatic harmonies which recall the improvisations of Turner rather than dispassionate observations of the modern school."[48]

Needing little to entice him to return to the Southwest, Akin went back to the Grand Canyon in 1905 with a SFRR commission to portray their most recent creation, the elegantly rustic El Tovar Hotel. While he would continue to travel east to visit, with this return Akin established his permanent home in Flagstaff. His painting, *El Tovar Hotel, Grand Canyon* (1906, p. 37), completed shortly after his arrival, emphasizes his familiarity with the place, providing a sweeping view not only of the approach to the structure and its imposing expanse, but also the spectacular view that it offers from its perch on the South Rim of the Grand Canyon. By bifurcating the composition Akin neatly contrasted the human and natural environments and, although his commission was to portray the hotel, the dominance of the trees in the foreground and the precipitous gorge that overwhelms the right half suggests that the hotel was of secondary importance to the artist. As in Moran's work before it, the sense of the canyon's power comprises the subject of the work, and like that artist's compositions too, this painting was reproduced by the SFRR and distributed through chromolithographs. It became one of Akin's most recognized images and remains a centerpiece of the SFRR collection today.

Despite Akin's success and that of those artists who followed him to the Grand Canyon, in the early years there was little market for paintings of a subject that was still unfamiliar to most Americans. Akin complained about this to William Simpson, "There are many things I can paint that sell better than Canyon pictures—probably nothing I could paint that would sell so slowly. But I've painted it because I am fascinated with it and because it is an achievement worth many vicissitudes."[49] He attempted to rectify this situation by painting in 1907 a huge six-by-nine-foot canvas of the canyon that would, he hoped, rival Moran's giant paintings from the 1870s. But the work was rejected by the National Academy of Design for its annual exhibition, and since it failed to sell afterward, the disappointed Akin kept it the rest of his life. In later years he designed murals for Southwestern exhibits at the American Museum of Natural History in New York (for which he consulted the aging Thomas Moran) and turned out a number of major paintings.[50] Although he died of pneumonia at an early age, he left a legacy of art and a profound love of the Grand Canyon and its peoples which would be an inspiration for all that would follow.

The next painter who would make the Grand Canyon his home was Swedish-born Gunnar Widforss (1879–1934). Early in the 1920s William Henry Holmes—the director of the National Gallery of Art in Washington and former pioneer artist of the Grand Canyon in his own right—suggested to Widforss, who was searching for a unique subject and style with which to make his mark, that he direct his attention to the landscape of the national parks. Awed by Yosemite, Widforss settled first in California, but after extensive travel throughout the West he made his home in the Grand

Canyon, living first with Emery and Ellsworth Kolb. Artists and pioneers themselves, the Kolb brothers had been living in the region since the 'teens, and were the first to attempt motion photography in the canyon in 1913. They recreated Powell's historic boat trip down the Colorado, taking one of the new cameras with them, ran a photo studio at the head of Bright Angel Trail, and served as guides to the area.[51]

Unlike other painters of the Grand Canyon who usually restricted their efforts to the rim of the chasm, Widforss took the trouble to traverse the arduous switchbacks of Bright Angel and other trails to create views from the floor of the canyon. Moreover, his favorite medium was watercolor rather than oil. The directness of the technique, and his skill in handling the sensitive nuances of tone and color, give his work a much stronger sense of immediacy and freshness than that of many other artists. He was enormously prolific, but both in his own time and to this day, his art remains underappreciated. The Santa Fe Railway bought a few of his works and many others were sold to tourists in the Fred Harvey shop at the El Tovar Hotel, but he was often forced to use his paintings as a medium of exchange, bartering them for food and clothing. Despite his lack of renown, however, Widforss's paintings rank with the very best of the art of the Grand Canyon, and deserve to be better known.[52]

Over the years other artists have made their home at the Grand Canyon, at least for a time. Warren Rollins had a studio at the El Tovar, for example, as did a number of artists who were especially favored by the Santa Fe company. More recently, Bruce Aiken (b. 1950) has made his home deep in the canyon and continues to paint from there. These fortunate individuals, who become as much a part of the place as it is of them, know the Grand Canyon as only natives can, and from them we gain special insight into its mysteries and unique visual language.

KOLB BEING LOWERED ON A ROPE, C. 1911
PHOTOGRAPH
CLINE LIBRARY,
UNIVERSITY OF NORTHERN ARIZONA

In this view the Kolb brothers demonstrate their daredevil negotiation of the Grand Canyon, for which they became locally famous. In 1913 they repeated John Wesley Powell's achievement of rafting the length of the Colorado River through the canyons, making history in their own right by being the first to take motion pictures of the journey. Later they set up a photography studio on the rim of the canyon and thrilled visitors with movies of their adventures.

LOUIS AKIN
MORNING—HERMIT CANYON, 1907
OIL ON CANVAS, 17 X 12 IN.
MUSEUM OF NORTHERN ARIZONA
FINE ARTS COLLECTION

LOUIS AKIN
THE RIVER, 1908
OIL ON CANVAS, 16 X 24 IN.
SANTA FE RAILWAY COLLECTION OF
SOUTHWESTERN ART

The sweep of our vision covers hun-
dreds of square miles of the Canyon—
an infinity of mountains, towers,
domes, spires, strange temples and
palaces, glowing with every conceivable
color, all marvelously distinct today,
distance alone softening the outlines
with a thin blue haze.
THOMAS D. MURPHY, 1913

LOUIS AKIN
EVENING—GRAND CANYON, N.D.
OIL ON CANVAS, 6 X 9 FT.
VERKAMP'S INC.
GRAND CANYON, ARIZONA

79

80

*My Grand Canyon pictures were received
by the press, critics, and the public with a
spontaneous approval and praise—putting
me away up in the front row of American
painters—in company that scares me
stiff—but I'll try to stay with them.*
—LOUIS AKIN, 1905

LOUIS AKIN
COLORADO RIVER, GRAND CANYON, 1911
OIL ON CANVAS, 30 X 20 IN.
SANTA FE RAILWAY COLLECTION OF
SOUTHWESTERN ART

82

I have seldom seen anything as bewitching as the purple and rose flames that glow in the canyon depths of those Western paintings.... To get those flame-and-mist tones Mr. Widforss must have dipped his brush in magic.
—EMILY GRANT HUTCHINGS, 1969

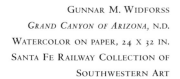

Gunnar M. Widforss
Grand Canyon, N.D.
Watercolor on paper, 21 x 28 in.
Collection of Michael and Leslie Engl, Sun Valley, Idaho
Courtesy of Zaplin-Lampert Gallery, Santa Fe, New Mexico

Gunnar M. Widforss
Colorado River, Grand Canyon, N.D.
Watercolor on paper, 18 x 21 in.
Arizona West Galleries, Scottsdale

For magnificent majesty, gorgeous coloring, and multiplicity of sculptured forms the Grand Canyon of the Colorado River has no rival in the world.
—George Wharton James, 1900

Gunnar M. Widforss
Grand Canyon of Arizona, 1924
Watercolor on paper, 29 1/2 x 25 in.
Arizona West Galleries, Scottsdale

All our previous standards of comparison must be revised; we have seen much of the world, but nothing to be fitly likened to this giant gorge.
—Thomas D. Murphy, 1913

87

Gunnar M. Widforss
Grand Canyon, 1924
Watercolor on paper, 20 x 16 in.
Arizona West Galleries, Scottsdale

88

GUNNAR M. WIDFORSS
KAIBAB FOREST, GRAND CANYON, 1921
WATERCOLOR ON PAPER, 25 X 19 IN.
PHOENIX ART MUSEUM
GIFT OF MRS. JOHN W. KIECKHEFER
IN MEMORY OF CAROLINE SMURTHWAITE FROM
FAMILY AND FRIENDS

GUNNAR M. WIDFORSS
PHANTOM RANCH, GRAND CANYON, 1925
WATERCOLOR ON PAPER, 21 X 24 IN.
SANTA FE RAILWAY COLLECTION OF
SOUTHWESTERN ART

MODERNISM AND THE GRAND CANYON

This is certainly no scene to be boggled by your sign-painting blockhead of an artist, with complacent reliance on his compasses and perspective scale, and paint pot and palette. There is a great tragic soul in the scene which the soul in the artist must clasp or fail utterly.
—Fitz-Mac [Fitz-James MacCarthy], 1906

As a result of the canyon's national park status in 1919 and the SFRR's increasingly visible advertising, tourism boomed at the Grand Canyon. At the same time as artists' communities such as those in Taos and Santa Fe were already developing their distinctive imagery, other artists were just beginning to discover the lure of the Southwest. Drawn by the region's elemental simplicity, its vivid color and light, many of these individuals were responding to a different aesthetic than the "Wild West" and its mythic associations. Infused with the new modernist sensibilities that were pervading the art world in the East and in Europe, many of these artists and writers recognized that modernism offered an alternative vision for their work, one that was in many ways perfectly suited to the unusual forms of the Grand Canyon.

You ask what attracted me to the Grand Canyon so far from my New England marshes. Color first of all— color 'burning bright' or smoldering under ash-grays. Then line—for the color lies in rhythmic ranges, pile on pile, a geologic Babylon. This high thin air is iridescent from cosmic dust: shapes and shadows seen in these vast distances and fearful deeps, are now blue, now vibrating with spectral hues. At sunset the 'temples' are flaming, red-orange—glorified like the Egyptian god in his sanctuary.
—Arthur Wesley Dow, 1913

ARTHUR WESLEY DOW
BRIGHT ANGEL CANYON, 1912
OIL ON CANVAS, 30 X 40 1/4 IN.
IPSWICH HISTORICAL SOCIETY,
IPSWICH, MASSACHUSETTS

Although the dominant mode of representing the Grand Canyon has been naturalistic throughout the twentieth century, the canyon's remarkable formations and vibrant colors have inspired an array of abstract treatments. Among the first of the artists to consider such an approach was Arthur Wesley Dow (1857–1922), a Massachusetts painter perhaps best remembered as a modernist who inspired Georgia O'Keeffe's early work. Dow visited the canyon in 1911–1912 with the photographer Alvin Langdon Coburn (1882–1966) and although his work was not unusually radical, in its theoretical foundation lay the beginnings of a new aesthetic form. Dow was influenced by Asian art throughout his career and incorporated much of the theory from Eastern visual practices into his own ideas. He especially appreciated the names of many of the canyon's peaks—Shiva's and Zoroaster Temples, for example—

and noted the compositional possibilities in the canyon's configurations. "It was this *line and color* that interested me," he wrote in an exhibition brochure, "hence I did not make any vague sketches. I wanted to seize the Grand Canyon's harmonies and these only. I hoped also to give the sense of vastness—the immense scale of everything there. In line the Grand Canyon is not unlike the classic subject of the Zen painters of China and Japan."[53] Dow's own work and his great legacy, conveyed through his practical book, *Compositions* (1899), which was widely used by art instructors, had its foundation in compositional theory based on abstraction from nature. In the Grand Canyon that abstraction seemed already realized, a modernist's vision in stone and light. As Dow wrote, "The Canyon is not like any other subject in color, lighting or scale of distances. It forces the artist to seek new ways of paint-

The Grand Cañon of the Colorado is a great innovation in modern ideas of scenery, and in our conceptions of the grandeur, beauty, and power of nature. As with all great innovations it is not to be comprehended in a day or a week, nor even a month. It must be dwelt upon and studied, and the study must comprise the slow acquisition of the meaning and spirit of that marvelous scenery which characterizes the Plateau Country, and of which the great chasm is the superlative manifestation.
—Clarence Dutton, 1882

Harry Paul Burlin
Grand Canyon, n.d.
Oil on canvas, 20 x 25 in.
The Harmsen Collection

ing—its own ways. Its record of the world's beginning holds for us the romance of geology."[54]

The following year, in 1913, another modernist, Paul Burlin (1886–1969), visited the Grand Canyon and was the first to apply the new notions of cubist form to the abstract elements inherent in the site. Burlin arrived shortly after his work had been exhibited in the famed Armory Show in New York, the first major exhibition of European modernism in the United States and a watershed in the history of American art. A friend of better-known painters such as Robert Henri and George Bellows, Burlin brought a new conception of visual imagery to the Grand Canyon, just as his New York friends would do throughout the Southwest at about the same time.[55] His forward-looking style was not only innovative for itself, but was also important for other artists in the area. "His studio [which he maintained in Santa Fe until 1920] was much sought by those who desired to get a glimpse of the most modern of modern art."[56] Just as the Colorado River had spent eons carving a most original work of art out of solid rock, so would artists finally arrive at a new way of seeing the Grand Canyon.

Although relatively few artists have taken full advantage of the Grand Canyon's abstract potential, Raymond Jonson (1891–1982) remains among the most dedicated to the region's formal properties. Although Jonson remains less well known than a number of his contemporaries, he made a major contribution to the art of the Southwest. His distinctive style, a decorative fusion of Cubism, Futurism, and Dynamic Symmetry, capitalized on the Canyon's dramatic geometry and dramatic colors and reconceived them into

new forms and arrangements. A professor of art at the University of New Mexico in Albuquerque, Jonson was staunchly progressive when, and where, aesthetic experimentation was unusual. From his earliest training at the Art Institute of Chicago and throughout his entire career, he was dedicated to modernist painting and the exploration of abstract visual form.

Jonson moved to Santa Fe in 1924 and after a visit to the Grand Canyon three years later wrote to his wife of his impressions: "It is immensely gorgeous—a hell of a hole in the ground full of detail and color—and infinite in variation. No one that I know of or anything I have seen expresses it at all. It is deep—high—concave—spacious—full of mystery and awesome. It is the strongest thing I have seen in nature. It is the most spiritual phenomenon of life I have seen—and it is inspiring."[57] This reaction was to have lasting implications for his art as he embarked on a series of multiple panel works abstracted from nature. The first, his monumental *Grand Canyon Trilogy* (1927), measuring thirteen feet in width, pushes the boundaries of representation, not only in its highly personal rhythmic style, but as well in its shaped central canvas and its triptych form which expands the visual field through multiple panels. A spiritual artist in all his work, in this painting Jonson drew upon the age-old religious configuration of altarpieces to unify the potentially disparate elements and endow the image with an intensified aura that would complement that of the subject itself. In such ways and in his influential teaching career Jonson was a major figure who paved the way for subsequent portrayals of the Grand Canyon.

RAYMOND JONSON
Grand Canyon Trilogy, 1927, oil on canvas, 36 x 45 in.
Bequest of Raymond Jonson, collection of the
Jonson Gallery, of the University of
New Mexico Art Museum, albuquerque

CONTEMPORARY VIEWS

This Grand Canyon of Arizona, and all the country surrounding it offers a new and comparatively untrodden field for pictorial interpretation, and only awaits the men of original thoughts and ideas to prove to their countrymen that we possess a land of beauty and grandeur with which no other can compare. The pastoral painter, and the painter of picturesque genre, the imaginative and dramatic landscapist are here offered all that can delight the eye, or stir the imagination and emotions.

—THOMAS MORAN, 1897

NAN CHAPIN ARCHILESI
*VINCENT ARCHILESI PAINTING
"THE GRAND CANYON" FROM THE NORTH RIM*, 1974
PHOTOGRAPH
COLLECTION OF THE ARTIST

THE ART of the Grand Canyon has never been more vibrant than today, at the end of the twentieth century. What began essentially in 1901 with the first artists' excursion has developed into a major tourist industry and a sophisticated art market, with dozens of painters annually visiting and working at the Grand Canyon. Some maintain the representational tradition of their predecessors; others are pushing the boundaries of pictorial form to new levels as they attempt to capture the dramatic essence of the great abyss. A few, like Louis Akin and Gunnar Widforss before them, make their home at the Grand Canyon, and more, like their counterparts who annually rode the Santa Fe rails to reach their cherished destination, visit from elsewhere. But whether they are traditional or innovative, residents or visitors, the contemporary artists of the Grand Canyon offer something for almost everyone as they portray the enduring "titan of chasms."

Although many artists avoided naturalistic subject matter in the 1950s and 1960s, favoring the dominant trends of abstraction and minimalism, the American landscape has reemerged in the last thirty years as an important artistic subject. Leading the resurgence in the mid 1970s was the U.S. Department of the Interior project *America 1976*, a program that offered grants to leading artists to paint landscapes in commemoration of the bicentennial anniversary of the United States.

Among the notable recipients of the grant was Philip Pearlstein (b. 1924) who traveled to the Grand Canyon in 1974. Already committed to what he called "New Realism," Pearlstein found new inspiration amid the ruins of the Southwest and its geological formations. "I've always been attracted to geology," he once said. "I'm happiest in museums, but the other time I'm really enthusiastic is when I'm in a ruin."[58] The ancient formations in the Grand Canyon had been likened to architecture since the days of the Spanish conquistadors, and these geological "ruins" offered Pearlstein a new subject at the same time as they evoked an epic past. His wash drawing, *Grand Canyon* (1975, p. 97), is typical of his site studies, which he would later transform into finished paintings. It shows his fascination with the terraces, bastions, and pinnacles of the rock walls and buttes. Although Pearlstein is better known for figurative work, especially his detailed portraits of nudes, his landscapes display many similarities to these paintings in their subtle color and their emphasis on contour and line, even as they are a direct response to the distinctive forms of the American Southwest.

Vincent Archilesi (b. 1932) also visited and painted the Grand Canyon through the *America 1976* project. A New Yorker noted for the variety of his subject matter and his realistic style, Archilesi, like Pearlstein, emphasizes the contours of the chasms and peaks more than their painterly and suggestive atmosphere.[59] Especially evident in the canvas he was photographed painting in 1974, the soft ochres and siennas transform mountains of rock into flesh-like folds and shadowed valleys more characteristic of a figure than rugged geology.

Quite removed from either architectural or anthropomorphic associations is the work of Clark Hulings (b. 1922), who has lived in Santa Fe since 1973. Slightly older than either Pearlstein or Archilesi and more traditional in his orientation to Southwestern art, Hulings continued the region's mythic association with the Old West in paintings such as *Grand Canyon-Kaibab Trail* (1976, p. 107). In this work, depicting a lone rider on his way up the famed historic pathway, the billowing remnants of a late-season snow heighten the textural effects of the surrounding rocks in a reminder of George Symons's winter work earlier in the century, and the figure evokes the strong Western tradition popularized by Charles Russell and Frederic Remington at the turn of the century.[60]

Many other recent artists in the Grand Canyon also draw strongly on historical precedents, both stylistically and thematically. Whether evoking nostalgia as in Huling's art, or the natural splendor of uninhabited scenes, the majority of these contemporary depictions of the Grand Canyon deliberately avoid or minimize the region's most dominant modern feature: the presence of humans. Preferring to contemplate the epic grandeur of the place as it would have appeared to the area's earliest visitors and inhabitants, these artists draw viewers' attention to the canyon's natural splendor, its remarkable expanse, ever-changing color and atmosphere, and its infinitude of detail. As Peter Nisbet (b. 1948) has said, "In my paintings I utilize a pictorial language set forth in past centuries simply because I believe that the highest standard of excellence for painting was set before the onset of the twentieth century."[61] The historic tradition of romantic and realist painting, such artists seem to say in their work, suits the enduring vistas of the Grand Canyon more effectively than more recent trends and artistic styles.

The work of Frank Mason (b. 1921) is perhaps the most rooted in academic tradition. A long-time painting instructor at the prestigious Art Students League in New York, he became known for his academically based methods and dedication to what he calls "traditional values" in art, drawing upon the old masters as much as any artist of the Grand Canyon since Moran. Not primarily a Southwestern painter, he is instead typical of Eastern artists in his European tendencies, but his annual summer courses in landscape painting in Vermont have provided an important basis for his own forays into the American West.

Different but just as historically reminiscent in their realist orientation are the works of Richard Iams (b. 1950) and Jerome Grimmer (b. 1939). Both utilize the centuries-old practice of applying translucent glazes to lend luminosity to their oils and acrylics. The resulting luminosity, accentuated by the palpable brushwork and implied glowing light, deepens the effect of space in the canyon views and positions their work with the best historic painting of the canyon.[62] Grimmer, who studied at the Art Center in Los Angeles and has worked as an illustrator, began painting professionally in 1975 and works exclusively in acrylics rather than oils, but he applies them in ways reminiscent of the grand tradition of oil painting. His early images focused on the oil fields of southern California, but he now lives in the foothills of the

Sierras and deals almost exclusively with more natural landscapes of the West. Although his work is extremely colorful, he says, "Some people think they must paint the Grand Canyon in a riot of color. I will use warm and subtle grays instead. If you compare my paintings of the Grand Canyon to theirs, you'd think I was color blind. But I want my buyers to be able to live with my paintings for many years."[63]

Iams, who has lived in Tucson since 1980, and visits and paints the canyon about four or five times a year, remarks,

> *The most difficult thing about painting the Grand Canyon is putting that much information and size onto whatever given board I'm working on. My paintings run a little big sometimes, but even that isn't enough size to do the canyon justice. Once you start painting the canyon, you don't stop; you keep going back to it . . . One of the most rewarding things I've had happen is to be at a show and see people walk in the door, look at one of my paintings of the Grand Canyon, freeze, and then take a step back. It's the realism. They get the sense of being there, that if they get too close they'll fall in.*[64]

As Iams and countless others have noted, in addition to color and texture, *space* is the Grand Canyon's most overwhelming characteristic. Although trained in abstraction with its ambiguous constructions of space, today's painters of the region attempt to objectify spatial qualities even more consciously than did their more romantic predecessors. Often they attempt this through painterly treatments reminiscent of the grand tradition of nineteenth-century landscape painting's sweeping vistas across the variegated horizon of the abyss. Recognizing, as painter Daniel Morper stated it, that "the sense of the Grand Canyon is better served by putting the viewer more immediately into its immense space," these artists are literally confrontational in their presentation of epic scale. But instead of alienating their audience, such works instead invite and intrigue, drawing us closer to the rocks, gorges, and peaks that were their source.

Ever since the heyday of the "big picture" in the 1860s artists have struggled to find equivalences for the epic scale of the American West. Thomas Moran addressed the problem early on in his monumental seven-by-twelve-foot canvas, *The Chasm of the Colorado*, but more recently artists have expanded their canvases even further, working into ever larger proportions and multiple panel images to approximate the grandeur of the Grand Canyon. Daniel Morper's four-panel *Point Sublime Panorama* (p. 120), Wilson Hurley's (b. 1924) three-part *October Suite, Grand Canyon* (1991, p. 132) and Peter Nisbet's (b. 1948) wide *Bradley Point* (1986, p. 142), for example, emphasize the panoramic spectrum of the subject in impressive formats that physically demonstrate the awe that virtually all visitors experience at the canyon.

Recasting the Renaissance notion of "windows on the world" into new forms, Morper, Hurley, and Nisbet draw upon the ancient concept of the sublime to elicit their viewers' response. Defined by that which prompts awe of the infinite, this notion is embodied in these canvases not only by their vast size, but by their exacting detail as well, an infinitesimal rendering of the parts that make up this most sublime of natural sites. Reviving the art of mural painting that was favored at the turn of the century and in the 1930s, these artists are engaging new audiences in the landscapes that are their inspiration, both through the fascinating minuteness of their visions and the epic scale of their creations.[65]

Two artists who address the Grand Canyon's unique qualities very differently are Ed Mell (b. 1942) and Angus MacPherson (b. 1952). Dealing in what has been called "the bones of nature," Phoenix native Mell concentrates on the masses of the Southwest's towering forms through smooth planes of color and an almost hard-edged linearity. Striking a balance between impact and intrigue as he negotiates the broadness of form and the harmonies of line, Mell recalls the work of Maynard Dixon or Georgia O'Keeffe and allows the scale of his work to express the raw beauty of the Western landscape. "Working on a large scale allows a landscape to have a lot of power," he has said about his work, and power is, in the end, the life force of his subject matter.[66]

MacPherson, by contrast, is more interested in atmosphere, in what he has termed the "chaos" of nature. In *Power of Wind and Water* (1989, p. 144) the atmosphere reigns over the rocks below, echoing John Wesley Powell, who wrote around the turn of the century, "At times, and perhaps in rare sensations, clouds and cloudlets form in the canyon below and wander among the side canyons and float higher and higher until they are dissolved in the upper air, or perhaps they accumulate to hide great portions of the landscape. Then through rifts in the clouds vistas of Wonderland are seen."[67]

The technical methods contemporary artists employ to capture their subject are as numerous as the artists themselves. Some are committed to direct observation and working *en plein aire* (outdoors) while others rely on photographs taken during travels through and around the Grand Canyon. These approaches not only reflect contemporary relationships to nature in their intentionality and conscious reliance on technology, but also a long tradition in American art that has sought the most effective and expedient means to encounter and record the landscape and its visual effects.

Thomas Moran used photographs to refine his paintings of the Grand Canyon as early as the 1870s, and many contemporary artists make this resource an integral component of their working process. William E. Porter (1931–1997), for example, freely admitted his reliance on slides and photographs for his prize-winning compositions, saying "I start by sketching real lightly on the paper, using the slide image cast by a two-by-two-foot rear projection screen."[68] Works such as his *Trimmed in Snow* and *Brahma Temple, Grand Canyon* (pp. 114–115) demonstrate that even as photorealism relies on the undeniable fidelity to the subject that only the camera can offer, the transformation of views into paint inevitably results in entirely different scenes, new visions that are both sharpened and clarified by their fixation in the photographic medium, but deepened through the sustained effort of

creation.[69]

Other artists work directly in nature, following in the tradition of the French Impressionists who took their canvases out of doors, *en plein aire*, to more spontaneously capture the fleeting effects of light and the atmosphere of the landscape and modern life. Sedona resident Curt Walters (b. 1950), for example, does nearly ninety percent of his painting on site at the canyon in order to more correctly observe the special characteristics of the place. "I'm one of those real nuts," he admits. "I stay through the harshest wind and rain. When the wind gets so severe that it's literally taking my canvas, I'll stop at that point. It's the same with rain. A hard rain will destroy my canvas."[70] He also takes photographs of his subjects throughout the day to provide references for refinements and finishing touches back in the studio, but even with these as backup his work is primarily drawn from direct observation.[71] In the tradition of *plein aire* work, his brush strokes are relatively broad and visually evident, indicative of the spontaneity of his Impressionist-derived approach.

While the most dramatic renditions of the Grand Canyon may be found in oil paintings, watercolors can be even more indicative of the region's translucent atmosphere and subtle color variations. In addition to William Porter, Colorado artist Merrill Mahaffey (b. 1937) is known for his work in the medium, and as such both artists may be said to follow in the footsteps of the watercolorist, Gunnar Widforss, earlier in the century. In such works as *Cliff Cascade* (p. 104) Mahaffey not only recalls the older artist's medium, but also Widforss's favorite point of view from the water's edge rather than the more lofty, and frequently painted scenery from the canyon's rim. As an avid Colorado River rafter, Mahaffey knows such sights well. His watercolors can either serve as preparatory studies for large murals or function as independent works of art.[72] Calling his early paintings from the canyon rim "cliches," he now focuses almost exclusively on the more intimate water view. John Wesley Powell, for all his early remarks on the evocativeness of the Grand Canyon from the rim, would have approved of these images, having once written, "When the Grand Cañon of the Colorado is painted the artist must stand by its raging waters and look up at its towering walls, and be overwhelmed by the gloomy grandeur of its depths."[73]

Perhaps the most intriguing characteristic of today's art of the Grand Canyon is its exquisite detail. Drawing on the documentary tradition of geological draughtsmen like William Henry Holmes, artists such as Earl Carpenter (b. 1931), Peter Holbrook (b. 1940), Bruce Aiken (b. 1950), John Cogan (b. 1953), and Mark Weber (b. 1949) emphasize to their viewers the subtle intricacies of the ancient forms. Just as John Wesley Powell, Clarence Dutton, and countless scientists have recognized that any true understanding of the canyon must derive from a comprehension of its myriad parts, so too do these artists convey the interconnectedness of strata in all their variety and power as they make up the seemingly infinite whole. Sacrificing nothing to total effect, in their attention to nuance these painters show us the real elements of the place—the rocks, the gullies, the walls, and the infinitesimal details that make up the enormity of the place.

Carpenter, a graduate of the Art Center in Los Angeles, moved to Arizona in 1960 and now lives near the Mogollon Rim. His early paintings were abstract, but like many other contemporary artists of the Southwest, he moved into Impressionist-based realism to convey the special characteristics of his landscape subject more convincingly. Like Monet and others before him working serially to explore a scene in its varying moods, light,

PHILIP PEARLSTEIN
GRAND CANYON, 1975
WASH ON PAPER, 29 1/2 X 41 IN.
UTAH MUSEUM OF FINE ARTS,
UNIVERSITY OF UTAH
PURCHASED WITH FUNDS FROM THE
CHARLES E. MERRILL TRUST AND THE NATIONAL
ENDOWMENT FOR THE ARTS, WASHINGTON, D.C.

97

Susan Shatter
Vertigo Black Canyon, 1981
Oil on canvas, 70 x 32 in.
Private collection
Courtesy Fischbach Galleries,
New York

and atmosphere more completely than in a single image, Carpenter often devotes several canvases to the same scene so "the full development of the idea can be realized."[74]

Peter Holbrook is another realist painter of the Grand Canyon. Currently a resident of Redway, California, his work has ranged widely since he received his B.A. from Dartmouth in 1961, from figurative imagery to landscape. Proficient in watercolor and other media, he contributed to the emergence of photorealism in the 1960s and the landscape revival of the 1970s and 1980s and has taught at a number of universities. His canyon scenes, like those of many of his contemporaries, explore the range of textures, patterns, colors, and detail of the canyon region through an accomplished facility with a variety of techniques, both historical and contemporary.

Bruce Aiken claims the unique position of actually living *in* his subject—as an employee of the National Park Service since 1973 he makes his home deep within the Grand Canyon near the pump station that supplies water to the canyon's north rim. From this enviable position he has the luxury of becoming intimately familiar with the canyon's changing seasons, moods, and intricacies, and this familiarity is embodied in his paintings. This isolation is not without its challenges; everything Aiken and his family of five needs, including food, has to be helicoptered to them. In order for the children to attend school, the family spends part of the year at the canyon's south rim. But the trade-offs have been worth it; the children have grown up surrounded by the beauty of one of the most remarkable areas on earth, and Aiken, who was raised in Manhattan and attended the Art Students League, is able to devote himself intensively to his subject. His paintings are strongly linear, with the attention to intricate detail more often found in watercolors, or in the highly topographical work of William Henry Holmes, one of the earliest survey artists in the canyon. At the same time, his unique circumstances distinguish his art from others'. As Aiken says, "It's not like I come here from Santa Fe, Albuquerque, Phoenix, or some other urban area, snap off a few pictures, do a couple of field pieces, and zoom back to town to throw the whole thing together in my studio. If I'm stumped, I can walk out the door and just take a peek."

John Cogan, a self-trained artist with a Ph.D. in physics from Rice University in Houston, derives the rich chromatic range in his paintings using a remarkably few pigments, namely the three primary colors—red, blue, and yellow—plus white. This derives in part from the palette of a childhood mentor, but may also reflect his own interest in the physical properties of pigments and their ability to combine optically into new form. Uniting scientific studies and a love of art to such a degree is rather unusual, but Cogan believes that "My background in science has been extremely helpful to my study of art: everything in the landscape is influenced by the physics of light, atmosphere, and optics. . . . When I paint the Grand Canyon, for instance, I am aware of the geology of the gorge and I am very interested in how the light affects the colors, forms, masses and voids. To me the painting that gets across the sense that there is light in the scene is the greatest accomplishment."[75]

Another Grand Canyon painter who focuses intently on light is Mark Weber. Reminiscent of the transcendent nineteenth-century canvases of Frederic Church, Sanford Gifford, or John F. Kensett with their displays of atmosphere through luminous ranges of color, Weber's paintings are suffused with the play of light and the clarity of form that results. Sometimes bordering on shocking color and brilliance, the scintillating canvases of this Kansas City resident distill ordinary views into the extraordinary, turning the remarkable into revelations.

Dennis Culver (b. 1945) had his early training at Chinouard at the Los Angeles Design Center and worked primarily in abstraction before moving to Santa Fe in 1969. Attracted to the light and color of the region and the potential it had for his palette, he moved away from abstraction into a more realist orientation, although he admits that his landscapes, while based in nature, are imbued with a strong sense of his own imagination. Although dedicated to landscape imagery, his work is varied; he works frequently with the figure and regularly participates in the John Sloan Drawing Group, an assemblage of professional artists who meet weekly to draw from the figure. Acknowledging that a single painted view can hardly contain the immensity of the Grand Canyon, Culver looks for small analogies, as in *Strata Various /Chasm* (p. 100), and focuses on geological detail and luminous surfaces.

Although the vast majority of contemporary paintings of the Grand Canyon are uninhabited, the presence of people in the region is an undeniable fact of modern life. With the flood of humanity visiting the site each year have come concerns about the fragile ecology of the Grand Canyon. A pressing issue that also dominates the entire contemporary American West, ecology figures prominently in artists' understanding of their subject and in their treatments of it. Curt Walters, for example, admitting "the helplessness I feel when confronted by the pollution which often surrounds the Canyon area," donates a portion of the proceeds from painting sales to the Grand Canyon Trust.[76] In the same spirit, the work of British artist Tony Foster (b. 1946) focuses on the ecological diversity of the region, almost as if his paintings were lessons in natural history. In visual montages such as *From the South Rim looking north over Indian Garden and Plateau Pont Rim. Four Days—April* (1988, p. 148) and *Slate Canyon to Boucher Creek* (1989, p. 149), Foster combines exquisite watercolor views with detailed specimen drawings and other details which offer both a macrocosmic and microcosmic consideration of the region and a different perspective on the natural life of the area. Mingling his vistas and panoramas with glimpses of the flora and fauna that inhabit the place, Foster simultaneously reminds viewers of the marvelous vitality of this ancient land and its fragility. Conceived as "watercolor diaries," or visual journals, the works frequently include inscriptions and maps, notations that mark specific places within this bewildering maze of canyons and gorges.[77] The natural history and the natural present comes alive in these sensitive images, offering us at once a view from within and without.

Woody Gwyn (b. 1944), by contrast, is intrigued as much by the human element in the most popular national park as by its natural forces. Like Oscar Berninghaus before him, who focused on the commercialization of the park and the flood of tourists that frequented it, Gwyn directs our attention to the interrelationship of humanity and nature in works such as *Tourists* (1989, p. 156). Emphasizing the contemporary experience of visiting and viewing this most popular of American scenic attractions, in this work Gwyn depicts a crowd sprinkled over a promontory that juts out over the yawning abyss. The visitors appear both arrogant and fragile against a shimmering blue backdrop of buttes and mesas, and are separated from the drop by only a delicate railing. The intensity of each, the human and the natural, Gwyn seems to be saying, is heightened by their juxtaposition. The power of the land is accentuated by the apparent fragility of the figures in contrast to it.[78] While this seems to make a powerful statement about the interaction of nature and culture, Gwyn has been quoted as saying that "Art has nothing to do with ideas, theories, or interpretation. I don't impose expectations anymore. Intellect has no place in art."[79] This would seem to preclude conclusions about the tense scene he presents at the Grand Canyon, but despite his anti-intellectualism, Gwyn's art does raise important issues that challenge the fragile ecosystem in the region.

Drawing from a very different tradition is the work of Alyce Frank, Susan Shatter (b. 1943), and Barbara Zaring (b. 1947).[80] All three of these women paint boldly rather than delicately, splashing their colors across the horizons in ways not unlike the sun as it daily paints the valleys and buttes of the Grand Canyon. Frank's and Zaring's work especially reminds viewers of that of Matisse with its brilliant chromatic spectrum, while Shatter's is slightly more subdued, but no less textural. As Zaring comments, "I'm walking a tightrope between realism and abstraction and there's no net. In one painting I may be totally non-objective, in another my imagery is more referential. It's satisfying, however, to find that abstract artists appreciate the representational imagery, and similarly realists relate positively to the non-objective work. I'll probably continue to go back and forth."[81] Recalling the age-old architectural metaphors that have been applied to the region, these artists conjure dramatic structures in their compositions, just as John Wesley Powell noted in his travels: "The whole scene is forever reminding you of mighty architectural pinnacles and towers and balustrades and arches and columns with latticework and delicate carving. All of these architectural features are sublime by titanic painting in varied hues—pink, red, brown, lavender, gray, blue and black. In some lights the saffron prevails, in other lights vermilion, and yet in other lights the grays and blacks predominate."[82]

Here is your country. Cherish these natural wonders, cherish the natural resources, cherish the History and Romance as a sacred heritage, for your children and your children's children. Do not let selfish men or greedy interests skin your country of its beauty, its riches, or its romance.

—PRESIDENT THEODORE ROOSEVELT, 1903

Merrill Mahaffey
Vishnu from the North, 1990
Watercolor on paper, 48 x 30 in.
Private collection

Merrill Mahaffey
Zoroaster with Brahma, 1987
Acrylic on canvas, 32 x 54 in.
Collection of the artist

Bruce Aiken
Full Force, 1989
Oil on canvas, 38 x 48 in.
Collection of the artist

Bruce Aiken
*Makin' the Pull at House
Rock Rapids*, 1981
Acrylic on canvas, 24 x 48 in.
Private collection

Merrill Mahaffey
Cliff Cascade, 1994
Watercolor on paper, 22 x 30 in.
Private collection

Among our parks, the Grand Canyon National Park in northern Arizona seems to be as unchanging as any of them. However, even a place like the Grand Canyon itself...is actually undergoing a constant change—change caused by nature and change caused by Man himself.
—WILLIAM J. BREED, 1976

107

CLARK HULINGS
GRAND CANYON—KAIBAB TRAIL, 1973
OIL ON CANVAS, 27 X 54 IN.
THE NATIONAL COWBOY HALL OF FAME AND
WESTERN HERITAGE CENTER,
OKLAHOMA CITY, OKLAHOMA
COURTESY OF THE ARTIST

The bright colors of the Canyon walls are stains from the various minerals and mineral salts originally in the sediments. The reds are known as ferrous oxides. It is interesting to note that the thickest stratum of all, about half way down the Canyon walls is known as 'red-wall limestone.' It was originallly a steel blue-gray in color. Its present red color is a mere superficial stain from the iron oxides of the formation directly above.

—Miner R. Tillotson and Frank J. Taylor, 1929

Frank Mason
Panorama of the Grand Canyon, 1983
Oil on canvas, 52 x 82 in.
The Winthrop Rockwood Family collection

Frank Mason
River View from Moran Point, 1983
Oil on canvas, 36 x 48 in.
The Winthrop Rockwood Family collection

110

RICHARD IAMS
WINTER SOLSTICE, 1988
OIL ON PANEL, 48 X 60 IN.
PRIVATE COLLECTION

Far below I hear a jumbled whistling, seething sound…It is the conflict of air currents among the narrow gorges.
And now, amid the tumult of sounds I begin to distinguish a new note.…With each sweep of the wind in my direc-
tion I catch it again, and each time, louder, wilder.…It is the roar of water, the thunder of many cataracts.

—WILLIAM R. LEIGH, 1909

RICHARD IAMS
WOTAN'S THRONE, NORTH RIM, 1990
OIL ON PANEL, 40 X 48 IN.
PRIVATE COLLECTION

112

CURT WALTERS
IMPETUOSITY, 1997
OIL ON CANVAS, 40 X 60 IN.
TRAILSIDE AMERICANA FINE ART GALLERIES,
SCOTTSDALE, ARIZONA

CURT WALTERS
UNRIVALED, 1995
OIL ON CANVAS, 50 X 80 IN.
TRAILSIDE AMERICANA FINE ART GALLERIES,
SCOTTSDALE, ARIZONA

*Today a new road, built only a few years ago, gives automobilists a glimpse into the
chasm as they approach. That spoils a bit of the drama, but perhaps it is just as well.
On my first visit a fellow traveler took one look and then ran back to throw his arms
around a tree. When I saw him last, he was desperately resisting the efforts of two
women companions to pry him loose.*
—JOSEPH WOOD KRUTCH, 1958

William E. Porter MWS

WILLIAM E. PORTER
CLEARING STORM, GRAND CANYON, 1991
WATERCOLOR ON PAPER, 30 X 22 IN.
COLLECTION OF JESSIE SMITH PORTER
COURTESY EL PRADO GALLERIES, INC.,
SEDONA, ARIZONA

WILLIAM E. PORTER
TRIMMED IN SNOW, 1991
WATERCOLOR ON PAPER, 22 X 30 IN.
COLLECTION OF JESSIE SMITH PORTER
COURTESY EL PRADO GALLERIES, INC.,
SEDONA, ARIZONA

116

JEROME GRIMMER
CANYON TWILIGHT, 1988
ACRYLIC ON CANVAS, 16 X 20 IN.
PRIVATE COLLECTION
COURTESY EL PRADO GALLERIES, INC., SEDONA, ARIZONA

Now, every sunlit desert morning has a magic moment. It may come at five o'clock, at seven, or at eleven, depending on the weather and the season. But it comes. If you are in the right mood at the right time, you are suddenly aware that the desert's countless cogs have meshed. That the world has crystallized into vivid focus. And you respond. You hold your breath or fall into a reverie or spring to your feet, according to the day and mood.
—COLIN FLETCHER, 1967

...there is nothing livable, nothing intimate about the Canyon. It is not a park or country-side scene, but a spectacle, a panorama— Nature in her most dramatic mood using her pageant properties with a prodigality of splendor almost unthinkable. It is a tremendous show, and to carry it off effects are employed that may be thought little short of theatrical.

—JOHN VAN DYKE, 1920

119

DANIEL MORPER
REUNION OF FOUR ELEMENTS, 1984
OIL ON CANVAS, 96 X 192 IN.
COLLECTION OF THE ARTIST

DANIEL MORPER
POINT SUBLIME PANORAMA, 1985
OIL ON PANEL, 4 PANELS, 32 X 44 IN. EACH (32 X 176 IN. TOTAL)
IBM COLLECTION

121

EARL CARPENTER
CANYON THUNDER, 1982
OIL ON CANVAS, 36 X 48 IN.
PRIVATE COLLECTION

In this dream I had found my way into an empty theater, one of those colossal and monstrous drama buildings, like the nightmare prisons that Piranesi drew...What I saw there was a real landscape, and I seem to remember feeling that this was not strange, considering the fabulous wealth and influence of this theater. But the scene itself was quite strange to me, [it] had some of the bright rock-coloring of Egypt and yet was not Egyptian. Now, looking at the Grand Canyon, I knew what I had seen, years before in that dream.

—J. B. PRIESTLY, 1937

EARL CARPENTER
YAKI POINT, N.D.
OIL ON CANVAS, 30 X 40 IN.
PRIVATE COLLECTION

124

PETER HOLBROOK

MORNING AT THE TOWER OF SET, 1995

OIL ON ACRYLIC ON CANVAS, 30 X 45 IN.

COLLECTION OF SKY HAREN

COURTESY OF THE ARTIST

There is a certain malady, commonly termed 'big head,' which a
large number of otherwise healthy people are afflicted.
Prescription: Stand upon the brink of the Grand Cañon, gaze
down, and still further down, into its awful depths, and realize
for the first time your own utter insignificance.

—MRS. MARY E. HART, M.D., 1895

PETER HOLBROOK

STORM OVER VISHNU TEMPLE, 1993

OIL ON ACRYLIC ON PAPER, 40 X 60 IN.

COLLECTION OF MIKE SHOLARS

COURTESY OF THE ARTIST

126

That beautiful haze, which tints, but does not obscure, enshrouded the temples and spires, changing from heliotrope to lavender, from lavender to deepest purple; there was a de-parting flare of flame like the collapse of a burning building; a few clouds in the zenith, torn by the winds so that they resembled the craters of the moon, were tinted for an instant around the crater's rims; the clouds faded to a dove-like gray; they darkened; the gray disappeared, the purple crept from the canyon into the arched dome overhead; the day was ended, twilight passed and darkness settled over all.

—E. L. KOLB, 1927

127

JOHN COGAN
LAST LIGHT HORUS TEMPLE, 1994
ACRYLIC ON CANVAS, 48 X 36 IN.
PRIVATE COLLECTION
COURTESY EL PRADO GALLERIES, INC.,
SEDONA, ARIZONA

Mark Christopher Weber

Rising Sun—Grand Canyon, 1995

Oil on panel, 24 x 36 in.

Collection of Gail Eberlein

Courtesy of the artist,

Kansas City, Missouri

Mark Christopher Weber

When the Mists Part, 1995

Oil on panel, 30 x 45 in.

Private collection

Courtesy of the artist,

Kansas City, Missouri

Mark Christopher Weber
Snow Castles, 1996
Oil on panel, 20 x 43 in.
Private collection
Courtesy of the artist,
Kansas City, Missouri

Mark Christopher Weber
Grand Canyon Lace, 1994
Oil on panel, 36 x 24 in.
Private collection
Courtesy of the artist,
Kansas City, Missouri

Those who have long and carefully studied the Grand Canyon of the Colorado do not hesitate for a moment to pronounce it by far the most sublime of all earthy spectacles. If its sublimity consisted only in its dimensions, it could be sufficiently set forth in a single sentence. It is more than two hundred miles long, from five to twelve miles wide, and from five thousand to six thousand feet deep. There are in the world valleys which are longer and a few which are deeper. There are valleys flanked by summits loftier than the palisades of the Kaibab. Still the Grand Canyon is the sublimest thing on earth. It is so not alone by virtue of its magnitudes, but by virtue of the whole—its tout ensemble.

—CLARENCE DUTTON, 1882

WILSON HURLEY
OCTOBER SUITE, GRAND CANYON, 1991
OIL ON CANVAS (TRIPTYCH), 72 X 90, 72 X 132, 72 X 90 IN.
EITELJORG MUSEUM OF AMERICAN INDIAN AND WESTERN ART,
INDIANAPOLIS, INDIANA

The buttes have the same coloring as the walls of the Canyon, only there is more of it—color on all sides instead of merely on a face-wall. And being in the round they catch more sunlight, throw off hues in more varied tones. But they have their times for splendor and are not uniformly brilliant from dawn to dusk. In fact, at noontime, with the sun overhead, they bleach out and their local hues are lost in the blue-grays. Noon is the worst possible hour at the Canyon, so far as color is concerned. Only at dawn or after sunset do the walls and buttes warm up and glow with hues both local and reflected.

—John Van Dyke 1920

134

WILSON HURLEY
ZOROASTER TEMPLE FROM MARICOPA POINT, GRAND CANYON, N.D.
OIL ON CANVAS, 60 X 90 IN.
COURTESY OF THE ARTIST

WILSON HURLEY
SUNRISE FROM EL TOWER, GRAND CANYON, N.D.
OIL ON CANVAS, 24 X 40 IN.
COURTESY NEDRA MATTEUCCI'S FENN GALLERIES,
SANTA FE, NEW MEXICO

137

I travel thousands of miles every year, and think I
have seen all the sights of the world. I have been
traveling for the past ten years. The Grand Cañon
of the Colorado River is the most wonderful piece of
work I have ever seen. Myself and Capt. John
Hance have been going for two days. Into the cañon
the first day, the rim the second. The most beautiful
view I think is from Moran Point.
—HERMAN D. OLESON, 1891

WILSON HURLEY
MORAN POINT, GRAND CANYON, 1978
OIL ON CANVAS, 40 X 80 IN.
COLLECTION OF THE ARTIST

138

PETER A. NISBET

WALL OF FIRE, 1988

OIL ON CANVAS, 24 X 18 IN.

COLLECTION OF THE ARTIST

PETER A. NISBET

STORM BREAK, GRAND CANYON, 1986

OIL ON CANVAS, 16 X 24 IN.

PRIVATE COLLECTION

The great barrier of the Canyon itself is only one of the many things which make the whole region one of the most astonishingly varied in America or, for that matter, anywhere else. Within a rectangle some two hundred miles long and a hundred miles broad there are differences of altitude totaling more than ten thousand feet and climates varying from the subtropical to the arctic. There are low, flat, burning deserts; there is a mighty river, and there are dark, volcanic peaks reaching nearly thirteen thousand feet above sea level. Scenically one may pass in less than an hour from one world to another which seems totally unrelated and pass at the same time from shirt sleeves to overcoat.

—JOSEPH WOOD KRUTCH, 1958

140

PETER A. NISBET
THE SADDLE, 1997
OIL ON CANVAS, 14 X 26 IN.
COLLECTION OF THE ARTIST

PETER A. NISBET
BRADLEY POINT, 1986
OIL ON CANVAS, 15 X 41 IN.
PRIVATE COLLECTION

Because we cannot relate ourselves to it, we remain outside, very much as we remain outside the frame of a picture. And though we may come back to a picture again and again, we cannot look at it continuously for any considerable period of time. To pass on to another picture is the almost inevitable impulse. And this is the reaction of a majority of visitors to the Canyon.
—JOSEPH WOOD KRUTCH, 1958

Angus MacPherson

Power of Wind and Water, 1989

Acrylic on canvas, 54 x 66 in.

Collection of Berry and Mary Lou Langford, New Mexico

Courtesy Dartmouth Street Gallery, Albuquerque

Ed Mell

Canyon Expanse, 1992

Oil on canvas, 48 x 78 in.

Collection of Mr. and Mrs. Robert Logan

*Stolid indeed is he who can front the awful scene and view its
unearthly splendor of color and form without quaking knee or
tremulous breath. An inferno, swathed in soft celestial fires; a whole
chaotic underworld, just emptied of primeval floods and waiting for
a new creative word; a boding terrible thing, unflinchingly real, yet
spectral as a dream eluding all sense of perspective dimension, out-
stretching the faculty of measurement, overlapping the confines of
definite apprehension...*
—C. A. HIGGINS, 1892

ED MELL
CANYON RIDGE, GRAND CANYON, 1993
OIL ON CANVAS, 26 X 36 IN.
PRIVATE COLLECTION

ED MELL
GOLDEN LIGHT, GRAND CANYON, 1993
OIL ON CANVAS, 18 X 27 IN.
PRIVATE COLLECTION

148

FROM THE SOUTH RIM LOOKING NORTH OVER INDIAN GARDEN & PLATEAU

KAIBAB LIMESTONE   TOROWEAP LIMESTONE · COCONINO SANDSTONE · HERMIT SHALE   SUPAI SHALE   REDWALL LIMESTONE   TEMPLE BUTTE LIMESTONE · MUAV LIMESTONE   BRIGHT ANGEL SHALE · TAPEATS SANDSTONE   SHINUMO QUAR

POINT · FOUR DAYS · APRIL

HAKATAI SHALE   BASS LIMESTONE   VISHNU SCHIST   ZOROASTER GRANITE

TONY FOSTER

FROM THE SOUTH RIM LOOKING NORTH OVER INDIAN GARDEN AND
PLATEAU PONT RIM. FOUR DAYS—APRIL 1989
WATERCOLOR AND ASSEMBLAGE ON PAPER, 57 3/4 X 28 1/4 IN.
COLLECTION OF THE ARTIST, CORNWALL, ENGLAND

149

...so many of these zones—as many as there are at sea level from Mexico to beyond the Arctic Circle—are so dramatically crowded together within the Canyon rectangle.... This concept of life zones is based upon the fact that climate is one of the most obvious of the things which determine the range, not merely of this or that particular plant or animal, but of an association or community of plants and animals often dependent upon one another as well as on the climate.

—JOSEPH WOOD KRUTCH, 1958

At the Grand Cañon the feeling of grandeur is not produced by power in activity, for the river is too far away, and forms too insignificant a part of the scene. Nor is it produced by the vastness of the chasm alone, for everyone has seen other things giving a more distinct impression of great extent or size. I think the feeling is one of awe and wonder at the evidence of some mighty, inconceivable, unknown power, at some time terribly, majestically and mysteriously energetic, but now ceased. And yet the force that has wrought so wonderfully through periods unknown, unmeasured, and unmeasurable, is a river 3000 feet below.

—JOHN COLBURN, 1872

150

SUSAN SHATTER
PIMA POINT, 1982
OIL ON CANVAS, 45 X 91 IN.
PRIVATE COLLECTION
COURTESY FISCHBACH GALLERIES, NEW YORK

Barbara Zaring
Moran Point, 1995
Oil on linen, 28 x 36 in.
Collection of Mr. and Mrs. R. Schuelke

Alyçe Frank
Bright Angel Overlook, 1995
Oil on canvas, 36 x 48 in.
Private collection

It seems that years ago, when this country was young and defenseless, some people more or less in authority broke in on the Canyon and exhausted the pantheon of gods in giving names to the buttes and promontories; and now everyone who talks or writes about the Canyon from necessity uses architectural terms and mythological names to point his meaning. The result is that these enormous Canyon forms are dwarfed to the building plan of a Buddhist temple and the great goddess Nature is put out of countenance by the blinking little divinities of India and Egypt.
—John Van Dyke, 1920

154

Barbara Zaring
Grand Canyon, Vishnu Temple, 1995
Oil on linen, 30 x 30 in.
Private collection

Alyce Frank
Moran Point, 1995
Oil on canvas, 24 x 36 in.
Private collection

EPILOGUE

The Grand Canyon of Arizona fills me with awe. It is beyond comparison—beyond description; absolutely unparalleled throughout the wide world....Let this great wonder of nature remain as it now is. Do nothing to mar its grandeur, sublimity and loveliness. You cannot improve upon it. But what you can do is to keep it for your children, your children's children, and all who come after you, as the one great sight which every American should see.
—President Theodore Roosevelt at the Grand Canyon, May 6, 1903

ALTHOUGH THE ART of the Grand Canyon as a whole takes us on a tour of the variety and magnificence of the place, even the best artists would agree that nothing can substitute for seeing it in person. Their work provides an almost endless array of insights, but even more varied is the place itself. No photograph, painting, journal, scientific report, or even memory can approach its grandeur, power, and mystery. In the words of an early twentieth-century writer, "All our previous standards of comparison must be revised; we have seen much of the world, but nothing to be fitly likened to this giant gorge."[84] But even as we admit their shortcomings, the paintings of the Grand Canyon approach as nothing else can the spectacle of the place. In their history, varieties of style, sincerity of intent, and sheer effect they give us a satisfying counterpart to the incomparable.

As we enter a new century and a new millenium, it seems only fitting that we contemplate the Grand Canyon anew. Just as the chasm itself reveals its origins in its walls of rock, opening itself to understanding and providing a lesson in our relationship to the earth and to time, so too do the painters offer their insights into both the place and its mysteries. As they distill their experiences into images of paint and canvas, watercolor and paper, they do more than capture the beauty of the place. They reflect back something of ourselves in those visions. We glimpse both our aspirations and our humility in the yawning gulf of that Grandest Canyon of them all.

156

Woody Gwyn
Tourists, 1989
Oil on canvas, 72 x 94 in.
Katharina Rich Perlow
Gallery, New York

The swarming of people to the Rim areas, onto the trails and adjacent wilderness, the river-running and attendant camping upon the River's banks and beaches, all directly contribute to changes of the Canyon by exposing previously inaccessible areas to heavy human traffic. Some of our man-made changes are obvious, while others are more subtle; how many times can a trailside or riverside plant be stepped upon before it dies?
—William J. Breed, 1976

NOTES

1. William Allen White, *McClure's Magazine* (September 1905).

2. Charles Higgins, *The Titan of Chasms* (Chicago: The Passenger Department of the Santa Fe Railway, 1897).

3. Other accounts place a variety of other individuals and government surveys in the region before Ives, but the facts on these are conflicting. See, for example, the maps in the authoritative book by William H. Goetzmann, *Exploration and Empire: The Explorer and the Scientist and the Winning of the West* (1966; reprint edition, Austin: Texas State Historical Association, 1993), compared to the numerous individuals given credit for being in the region by George Wharton James in *In & Around the Canyon: The Grand Canyon of the Colorado River in Arizona* (Boston: Little, Brown and Company, 1900), pp. 11–19. For a more thorough discussion, see David Lavender, *Colorado River Country* (New York: E. P. Dutton, 1982), pp. 32–77.

4. Egloffstein had been with John Charles Frémont and Lieutenant Beckwith in Utah, and Möllhausen had been with Lieutenant Whipple in southern Arizona, both in 1853.

5. Lieutenant Joseph Christmas Ives, *Report Upon the Colorado River of the West*, Senate Executive Document, 36th Congress, 1st Session, 1861, p. 99.

6. Ben Huseman, *Wild River, Timeless Canyons: Balduin Möllhausen's Watercolors of the Colorado* (Fort Worth: Amon Carter Museum, distributed by University of Arizona Press, 1995).

7. Powell's writings have been reprinted in a variety of forms, but the most important is his final report on the river system: John Wesley Powell, *Exploration of the Colorado River of the West and Its Tributaries: Explored in 1869, 1870, 1871, and 1872, Under the Direction of the Secretary of the Smithsonian Institution* (Washington: U.S. Government Printing Office, 1875). He wrote of his adventures in more popular form in *Canyons of the Colorado* (1895), reprinted as *Explorations of the Colorado River and Its Canyons* (New York, 1961).

8. For more on Powell see the classic biography by Wallace Stegner, *Beyond the Hundredth Meridian: John Wesley Powell and the Second Opening of the West* (New York: Houghton Mifflin, 1953).

9. Frederick Dellenbaugh's works includes *A Canyon Voyage: The Narrative of the Second Powell Expedition Down the Green-Colorado River from Wyoming, and the Explorations on Land in the Years 1871 and 1872* (New York, 1908); *Breaking the Wilderness: The Story of the Conquest of the Far West, From the Wanderings of Cabeza de Vaca to the First Descent of the Colorado by Powell and the Completion of the Union Pacific Railway* (New York, 1905); and *Romance of the Colorado River: The Story of Its Discovery in 1540, with an Account of the Later Explorations, and with Special Reference to the Voyages of Powell Through the Line of the Great Canyons* (New York, 1902).

10. The two paintings hung across from each other in the Capitol until the middle of the twentieth century, when the Senate press corps moved into their hall. They were transferred to the Department of the Interior and then in 1968 were permanently loaned to the National Museum of American Art, where they remain today.

11. This explains why the images in both the *Scribner's* articles and the Powell report are identical. For more see Joni L. Kinsey, *Thomas Moran and the Surveying of the American West* (Washington and London: Smithsonian Institution Press, 1992).

12. Powell, *Exploration of the Colorado River of the West and its Tributaries*, p. 174.

13. Richard Watson Gilder, "Culture and Progress: 'The Chasm of the Colorado,'" *Scribner's Monthly* 8 (July 1874): 373.

14. Thomas Moran, "American Art and American Scenery," in Charles Higgins, ed., *The Grand Canyon of Arizona* (Chicago: The Passenger Department of the Santa Fe Railway, 1906), p. 87.

15. For more on Colman see Patricia Trenton and Peter Hassrick, *The Rocky Mountains: A Vision for Artists in the Nineteenth Century* (Norman: University of Oklahoma Press, 1983), pp. 238–39.

16. Clifford Nelson, "William Henry Holmes: Beginning a Career in Art and Science," *Records of the Columbia Historical Society* 50 (1980): 252–78, and Amy Batson Strange, "William Henry Holmes, Artist," M.A. thesis, University of Florida, 1992.

17. For more on this see my *Thomas Moran*, chapters three and four, and more generally, Alfred Runte, *Trains of Discovery: Western Railroads and the National Parks* (Niwot, Colorado: Roberts Rinehart, Inc., 1990).

18. The history of the company has been most thoroughly documented by Keith Bryant, *History of the Atchison, Topeka, and Santa Fe Railway* (Lincoln and London: University of Nebraska Press, 1974). For its relationship with artists see Bryant, "The Atchison, Topeka, and Santa Fe Railway and the Development of the Taos and Santa Fe Art Colonies," *Western Historical Quarterly* 9 (October 1978): 437–54, and more recently Sandra D'Emilio and Suzan Campbell, *Visions and Visionaries: The Art and Artists of the Santa Fe Railway* (Salt Lake City: Peregrine Smith Books, 1991).

19. General Advertising Agent (William H. Simpson) to J. M. Connell, 22 January 1915. Moran curatorial file, Santa Fe Railway Collection of Southwest Art, Chicago.

20. Edward Hungerford, "Consistent Railroad Advertising," *The Santa Fe Magazine* 19 (March 1923): 44–48; cited in D'Emilio and Campbell, *Visions and Visionaries*, p. 17.

21. Newspaper notice, *Williams News* (Arizona) 9 (Saturday, May 25, 1901): 2.

22. In 1910, for example, the artists' excursion group consisted of Gustave Buek (who had been the engraver for the 1892 Moran Grand Canyon painting the Santa Fe reproduced), Elliott Daingerfield, Ballard Williams, Edward Potthast, and DeWitt Parshall. See Nina Spaulding Stevens, "Pilgrimage to the Artist's Paradise," *Fine Arts Journal* (February 11, 1911): 105–117, and Gustave Kobbe, "Artists Combine for a Trip to Arizona," *New York Herald* (November 26, 1911).

23. Many of the visitors to the Grand Canyon recorded their thoughts about the place in the visitors' book kept by Captain John Hance, one of the early residents of the area and noted guide in the late nineteenth and early twentieth century. The list reads like a virtual "who's who" of the region in the early days. The book has been published by G. K. Woods, ed. *Personal Impressions of the Grand Cañon of the Colorado River Near Flagstaff, Arizona* (San Francisco: The Whitaker & Ray Co., 1899).

24. William R. Leigh, "Impressions of an Artist while Camping in the Grand Canyon, Arizona," unpublished manuscript. Cited in June DuBois, *W. R. Leigh: The Definitive Illustrated Biography* (Kansas City: The Lowell Press, 1977), p. 57.

25. Ibid, p. 59.

26. Ibid, pp. 59–60.

27. Dubois, *W. R. Leigh*, p. 68, and Kinsey, *Thomas Moran*, p. 113.

28. See Stevens, "Pilgrimage to the Artist's Paradise," and Kobbe, "Artists Combine for a Trip to Arizona." *New York Herald*. Stevens credits Buek with the idea of the excursion, p. 107.

29. Stevens, "Pilgrimage to the Artist's Paradise," p. 107.

30. Ibid, p. 108.

31. Ibid, p. 113.

32. William Gerdts, *American Impressionism* (New York: Artabras, 1984), pp. 244–45.

33. Cited in Robert Hobbs, *Elliott Daingerfield Retrospective Exhibition* (Charlotte, North Carolina: Mint Museum of Art, 1971), p. 48. Daingerfield wrote a number of art reviews and essays on art and aesthetics. Hobbs's book contains a listing of these.

34. See also Estill Curtis Pennington and J. Richard Gruber, *Victorian Visionary: The Art of Elliott Daingerfield* (Augusta, Georgia: Morris Museum of Art, 1994). The Morris Museum of Art owns over one hundred paintings and works on paper by Daingerfield.

35. Gordon E. Sanders, *Oscar Berninghaus, Taos New Mexico: Master Painter of American Indians of the Frontier West* (Taos, New Mexico: Taos Heritage, 1985).

36. For more on Blumenschein see William T. Henning Jr., *Ernest L. Blumenschein Retrospective* (Colorado Springs: Colorado Springs Fine Art Center, 1978); and Charles C. Eldredge, Julie Schimmel, and William H. Truettner, *Art in New Mexico, 1900–1945: Paths to Taos and Santa Fe* (New York: Abbeville Press for the National Museum of American Art, 1986).

37. Borg actually spent a good part of his time until 1925 traveling throughout the Southwest, to Central America, and to Europe before he finally settled in Los Angeles. For more on Borg see Katherine Plake Hough, Michael R. Grauer, and Helen Laird, *Carl Oscar Borg: A Niche in Time* (Palm Springs: Palm Springs Desert Museum, 1990); Katherine Plake Hough, "Carl Oscar Borg," *Southwest Art* 19 (April 1990): 67–73; and Helen Laird, *Carl Oscar Borg and the Magic Region: Artist of the American West* (Layton, Utah: Gibbs Smith, Inc., 1986).

38. Quoted in Laird, *Carl Oscar Borg*, p. 113.

39. Both paintings are also extremely similiar in their composition to a pre-1920 photograph copyrighted by Fred Harvey that may have been offered for sale at the Harvey hotels. This view is reproduced and identified in John C. Van Dyke, *The Grand Canyon of the Colorado: Recurrent Studies in Impressions and Appearances* (New York: Charles Scribner's Sons, 1920), facing p. 140.

40. J. Donald Hughes, *The Story of Man at the Grand Canyon* (Grand Canyon: National Park Service, 1967), pp. 116–17.

41. Rena Neumann Coen, "Edgar Alwin Payne," *Southwest Art* 19 (October 1989): 96–102, 242, 244.

42. Little has been written about Jacobson, but his activities are well documented in the archives of the University of Oklahoma.

43. Gerdts, *American Impressionism*, pp. 235-36.

44. Robert S. Olpin, "Tradition and the Lure of the Modern: 1900–1950," in Vern G. Swanson, Robert S. Olpin, and William C. Seifrit, *Utah Art* (Layton, Utah: Peregrine Smith, 1991), 119. See also Erica Doss, "'I Must Paint': Women Artists of the Rocky Mountain Region," in Patricia Trenton, ed., *Independent Spirits: Women Painters of the American West, 1890–1945* (Berkeley and Los Angeles: Autry Museum of Western Heritage in association with the University of California Press, 1995), p. 224.

45. See Sarah Moore, "No Woman's Land: Arizona Adventurers," in Trenton, ed., *Independent Spirits*, pp. 131–51 and also Donald J. Hagerty, *Desert Dreams: The Art and Life of Maynard Dixon* (Layton, Utah: Peregrine Smith Books, 1993).

46. William Balken, *Six Mois Aux Etats Unis: The Drawings of Albert Tissandier* (Provo: Utah Museum of Fine Arts, University of Utah, 1986).

47. The Utah Museum of Fine Arts in Provo owns 220 of Tissandier's drawings from his 1885 trip to the United States.

48. Cited in Bruce E. Babbitt, *Color and Light: The Southwest Canvases of Louis Akin* (Flagstaff, Arizona: Northland Press, 1973), p. 17.

49. Ibid., p. 23.0

50. Ibid., pp. 23–30, 57.

51. The Kolb expedition is described in E. L. Kolb (with a foreword by Owen Wister) *Through the Grand Canyon From Wyoming To Mexico* (New York: MacMillan Co., 1927).

52. To date the only significant study of Widforss is Bill Belknap, and Frances Spencer Belknap, *Gunnar Widforss, Painter of the Grand Canyon* (Flagstaff: Northland Press, for the Museum of Northern Arizona, 1969).

53. Arthur Wesley Dow, "Notes on my Paintings of the Grand Canyon of Arizona." Typescript manuscript to accompany exhibition at the Montross Gallery, New York, April 7–19, 1913. Cited in Ballinger and Rubinstein, *Visitors to Arizona*, p. 28.

54. Arthur Wesley Dow, "The Color of the Grand Canyon," introduction to *The Color of the Grand Canyon of Arizona. Exhibition of Pictures by Arthur Wesley Dow, April 7 to April 19, 1913* (New York: Montross Gallery, 1913). For more on Dow see Frederick C. Moffatt, *Arthur Wesley Dow (1856–1922)* (Washington: Smithsonian Institution Press for the National Collection of Fine Arts, 1977), esp. pp. 119–21.

55. For more on this see Patricia Janis Broder, *The American West: The Modernist Vision* (Boston: New York Graphic Society, 1984).

56. Quoted in Van Deren Coke, *Taos and Santa Fe: The Artist's Environment, 1882–1942* (Albuquerque: University of New Mexico Press, for Amon Carter Museum of Western Art and Art Gallery, 1963), p. 31.

57. Quoted in Ed Garman, *The Art of Raymond Jonson* (Albuquerque: University of New Mexico Press, 1976), pp. 194–95. The University of New Mexico's Jonson Gallery owns over 670 works by Jonson.

58. Quoted in Russell Bowman, *Philip Pearlstein: The Complete Paintings* (New York and London: Alpine Fine Arts Collection, Ltd., 1983), p. 8.

59. For more on Archilesi see John Arthur, *Spirit of Place: Contemporary Landscape Painting and the American Tradition* (Boston: Bullfinch Press and Little, Brown & Co., 1989).

60. Peggy and Harold Samuels, *Contemporary Western Artists* (New York: Bonanza Books, 1982), p. 269.

61. "P. A. Nisbet: New Paintings, August 11–September 5, 1995." Manuscript accompanying Nisbet exhibition at Frank Croft Fine Art Gallery, Santa Fe.

62. J. Darrell Beach, "Richard Iams," *Southwest Art* 18 (February 1989): 76–82; Kate Ruland-Thorne, "Jerome Grimmer," *Southwest Art* (October 1988): 80–85.

63. Ruland-Thorne, "Jerome Grimmer," *Southwest Art* (October 1988): 85.

64. Behrens, Shirley, "Richard Iams: Instilling a Greater Truth," *Art of the West* (January/February 1993).

65. Karen Klinka, "Wilson Hurley: Windows of the West," *Southwest Art* 24 (November 1994): 48–53; Nancy Ellis, "In Search of the Deep and Meaningful: The Landscape Art of Peter Nisbet," *Focus/Santa Fe* (June–July 1989): 32–35; Joy Waldron Murphy, "P. A. Nisbet: Yearning for Place," *Southwest Art* (August 1987): 60–56. For Hurley, see also Samuels, *Contemporary Western Artists*, p. 270.

66. Barbara Cortright, "The Bones of Nature," *Southwest Profile* (March 1990): 27–30.

67. John Wesley Powell, "The Scientific Explorer," in *The Grand Canyon of Arizona* (Chicago: The Passenger Department of the Santa Fe Railway, 1906), p. 26.

68. Quoted in David Hale, "National Park Grand Prize a Natural Wonder to Artist," *Fresno Bee* (September 30, 1990): F24. The recipient of numerous awards for his art, William Porter won the $50,000 Art for the Parks Prize in

1990 for a Grand Canyon scene, *Escalante Butte*, a watercolor. Porter, represented by El Prado Galleries Inc., in Santa Fe and Sedona, grew up in Oklahoma, graduated from Fresno State in the mid-1950s with a degree in art and then served in the Air Force until 1981, when he resumed painting professionally full time.

69. For a discussion of photorealism within modern western art see Broder, *The American West*, pp. 314–29.

70. Dawn DeVries, "Going to Extremes: Curt Walters is Dedicated to Capturing Nature on Canvas." *Scottsdale Progress, Scottsdale Life* (February 18, 1993): 2.

71. Becky Ramsdell, "The Ultimate Landscape: Sedona Painter Hooked on Grand Canyon," *Arizona Daily Sun* (Flagstaff, March 21, 1996): A4. Walters studied art at New Mexico State University and worked as struggling painter in Taos in the 1970s during which time he began taking short trips to the Grand Canyon. See Samuels, *Contemporary Western Artists*, p. 560.

72. Mahaffey's large mural work may be found in the Phoenix airport and the Chandler Fine Arts Complex in Arizona. For more on Mahaffey see Stanley L. Cuba, "Merrill Mahaffey," *Southwest Art* 22 (September 1992): 70–76; and Stephen Parks, "Grand Paintings of the Canyon," *Southwest Profile* (February 1990): 23–26.

73. John Wesley Powell, unidentified clipping, Thomas Moran Papers, Archives of American Art, NTM 4, frame 608.

74. Samuels, *Contemporary Western Artists*, p. 96.

75. Netta Pfeifer, "John Cogan," *Southwest Art* (October 1989): 125–28.

76. "A Grand Stroke for the Grand Canyon," *Monterrey Bay* (September–October 1994): 38; and James Bishop Jr. "Captured In the Colors," *Phoenix Magazine* (June 1995): 92–96.

77. *Tony Foster: Exploring the Canyon, Watercolour Diaries, 1988–1989* (Penzance, England: Newlyn Orion Galleries in association with Montgomery Gallery, San Francisco, 1989).

78. Lisa Sherman, "Woody Gwyn," *Artspace* 7 (Winter 1982–83): 39–42.

79. Samuels, *Contemporary Western Artists*, p. 233.

80. Martha Burnett Goodwin, "Alyce Frank," *Southwest Art* 21 (November 1991): 71–76; Nancy Gillespie, "Barbara Zaring Thayer," *Southwest Art* 19 (December 1989): 64–69. Susan Shatter is represented by Fischbach Galleries in New York.

81. Quoted in Gillespie, "Barbara Zaring Thayer," pp. 68–69.

82. John Wesley Powell, "The Scientific Explorer," in *The Grand Canyon of Arizona*, p. 26.

83. Thomas D. Murphy, *Three Wonderlands of the American West* (Boston: L. C. Page & Co., 1913), pp. 115–116.

SELECTED BIBLIOGRAPHY

Babbitt, Bruce E. *Color and Light: The Southwest Canvases of Louis Akin*. Flagstaff, Arizona: Northland Press, 1973.

Ballinger, James K., and Andrea D. Rubenstein. *Visitors to Arizona 1846 to 1980*. Phoenix: Phoenix Art Museum, 1980.

Beach, J. Darrell. "Richard Iams." *Southwest Art* 18 (February 1989): 76–82.

Belknap, Bill, and Frances Spencer Belknap. *Gunnar Widforss, Painter of the Grand Canyon*. Northland Press, for the Museum of Northern Arizona, 1969.

Bermingham, Peter. *The New Deal in the Southwest: Arizona and New Mexico*. Tucson: University of Arizona Museum, 1980.

Broder, Patricia Janis. *The American West: The Modern Vision*. New York and Boston: New York Graphic Society and Little, Brown and Company, 1984.

Bryant, Keith. "The Atchison, Topeka, and Santa Fe Railway and the Development of the Taos and Santa Fe Art Colonies." *Western Historical Quarterly* 9 (October 1978): 437–54.

_____. *History of the Atchison, Topeka, and Santa Fe Railway*. Lincoln and London: University of Nebraska Press, 1974.

Burnside, Welsey M. *Maynard Dixon: Artist of the West*. Provo: Brigham Young University Press, 1974.

Coen, Rena Neumann. "Edgar Alwin Payne." *Southwest Art* 19 (October 1989): 96–102, 242, 244.

Cuba, Stanley L. "Merrill Mahaffey." *Southwest Art* 22 (September 1992): 70–76.

Curtis, Natalie, "A New Art in the West." *The International Studio* 63 (November 1917)

Dellenbaugh, Frederick. *A Canyon Voyage: The Narrative of the Second Powell Expedition Down the Green-Colorado River from Wyoming, and the Explorations on Land in the Years 1871 and 1872*. New York, 1908.

_____. *Breaking the Wilderness: The Story of the Conquest of the Far West, From the Wanderings of Cabeza de Vaca to the First Descent of the Colorado by Powell and the Completion of the Union Pacific Railway*. New York, 1905.

_____. *Romance of the Colorado River: The Story of Its Discovery in 1540, with an Account of the Later Explorations, and with Special Reference to the Voyages of Powell Through the Line of the Great Canyons*. New York, 1902.

D'Emilio, Sandra, and Suzan Campbell. *Visions and Visionaries: The Art and Artists of the Santa Fe Railway*. Salt Lake City: Peregrine Smith Books, 1991.

Dubois, June. *W. R. Leigh: The Definitive Illustrated Biography*. Kansas City: The Lowell Press, 1977.

Dutton, Clarence E. *The Physical Geology of the Grand Cañon District*. Washington, 1882.

_____. *Tertiary History of the Grand Canyon District and Atlas*. Washington, 1882.

Eldredge, Charles C., Julie Schimmel, and William H. Truettner. *Art in New Mexico, 1900–1945: Paths to Taos and Santa Fe*. New York: Abbeville Press for the National Museum of American Art, 1986.

Fowler, Don D. *The Western Photographs of John K. Hillers*. Washington and London: Smithsonian Institution Press, 1989.

Garman, ed. *The Art of Raymond Jonson, Painter*. Albuquerque: University of New Mexico Press, 1976.

Gillespie, Nancy. "Barbara Zaring Thayer." *Southwest Art* 19 (December 1989): 64–69.

Goetzmann, William H. *Exploration and Empire: The Explorer and the Scientist and the Winning of the West*. 1966; reprint edition, Austin: Texas State Historical Association, 1993.

Goodwin, Martha Burnett. "Alyce Frank." *Southwest Art* 21 (November 1991): 71–76.

The Grand Canyon of Arizona. Chicago: The Passenger Department of the Santa Fe Railway, 1906.

The Grand Canyon of Arizona: Being a Book of Words From Many Pens, About the Grand Canyon of the Colorado River In Arizona. Chicago: The Passenger Department of the Santa Fe Railway, 1909.

Hamlin, Edith. "Maynard Dixon: Painter of the West." *American West* 19 (November/December 1982): 50–58.

Henning, William T. Jr. *Ernest L. Blumenschein Retrospective*. Colorado Springs: Colorado Springs Fine Art Center, 1978.

Higgins, Charles A. *The Grand Cañon of the Colorado River*. Chicago: The Passenger Department of the Santa Fe Railway and The Henry O. Shepherd Co., 1892, 1897.

_____. *Titan of Chasms: The Grand Canyon of Arizona*. Chicago: The Passenger Department of the Santa Fe Railway, 1905.

_____, ed. *The Grand Canyon of Arizona*. Chicago: The Passenger Department of the Santa Fe Railway, 1906.

Hobbs, Robert. *Elliot Daingerfield Retrospective Exhibition*. Charlotte, North Carolina: Mint Museum of Art, 1971.

Hough, Katherine Plake. "Carl Oscar Borg." *Southwest Art* 19 (April 1990): 67–73.

Hough, Katherine Plake, Michael R. Grauer, and Helen Laird. *Carl Oscar Borg: A Niche in Time*. Palm Springs: Palm Springs Desert Museum, 1990.

Hughes, J. Donald. *The Story of Man at the Grand Canyon*. Grand Canyon: National Park Service, 1967.

Huseman, Ben. *Wild River, Timeless Canyon: Balduin Mollhausen's Watercolors of the Colorado*. Fort Worth: Amon Carter Museum, distributed by University of Arizona Press, 1995.

Ingersoll, Ernest. *The Crest of the Continent: A Record of A Summer's Ramble in the Rocky Mountains and Beyond*. Chicago: R. R. Donnelley & Sons, 1888.

Ives, Joseph Christmas. *Report Upon the Colorado River of the West*. Senate Executive Document, 36th Congress, 1st Session, 1861.

Jacobwitz, Arlene. *Edward Henry Potthast, 1846–1927*. New York: The Chapellier Galleries, 1969.

James, George Wharton. *In & Around the Canyon: The Grand Canyon of the Colorado River in Arizona*. Boston: Little, Brown and Company, 1900.

Johnson, Bonnie, and Toff Gold. "Peace in a Lonley Place," *People Magazine* (October 21, 1991): 107–108.

Budge Ruffner. "Bruce Aiken: From the Bottom," *Southwest Art* (November 1987): 39–44.

Jonson, Raymond. "The Role of Abstract Art." *El Palacio* 48 (March 1941): 62–70.

Kinsey, Joni Louise. *Thomas Moran and the Surveying of the American West*. Washington and London: Smithsonian Institution Press, 1992.

Klinka, Karen. "Wilson Hurley: Windows of the West." *Southwest Art* 24 (November 1994): 48–53.

Kolb, E. L., with a foreword by Owen Wister. *Through the Grand Canyon From Wyoming To Mexico*. New York: Macmillan, 1927.

Laird, Helen. *Carl Oscar Borg and the Magic Region*. Layton, Utah: Peregrine Smith Books, 1986.

Lavender, David. *Colorado River Country*. New York: E. P. Dutton, 1982.

Leavitt, Virginia Couse. "Eanger Irving Couse." *Southwest Art* 21 (December 1991): 76–85.

Lewisohn, Edna Manley. "Raymond Jonson: Painter." *El Palacio* 54 (May 1947): 111–15.

Lummis, Charles. "The Artist's Paradise." *Out West* 29 (Sept. 1908): 451; 29 (Sept. 1908): 174–91.

_____. *The Land of Poco Tiempo*. New York: Charles Scribner's Sons, 1893.

McCauley, Elizabeth Anne. *Raymond Jonson: The Early Years*. Albuquerque: University Art Museum, University of New Mexico, 1980.

McCutcheon, John T. *Doing the Grand Canyon*. New York: D. Appleton & Co., 1909; reprint edition, Chicago: Fred Harvey, 1922.

Miller, Arthur, introduction. *Maynard Dixon: Painter of the West*. Tuscon: Edith Hamlin Dixon, 1945.

Moffatt, Frederick C. *Arthur Wesley Dow (1856–1922)*. Washington: Smithsonian Institution Press for the National Collection of Fine Arts, 1977.

Morand, Anne R., Joni L. Kinsey, and Mary Panzer. *Splendors of the American West: Thomas Moran's Art of the Grand Canyon and Yellowstone*. Birmingham: Birmingham Museum of Art in association with University of Washington Press, 1990.

Murphy, Thomas D. *Three Wonderlands of the American West*. Boston, L. C. Page & Co., 1912.

Nelson, Clifford M. "William Henry Holmes: Beginning a Career in Art and Science." *Records of the Columbia Historical Society* 50 (1980): 252–78.

Pfeifer, Netta. "John Cogan." *Southwest Art* (October 1989): 124–128.

Powell, John Wesley. *Exploration of the Colorado River of the West and Its Tributaries: Explored in 1869, 1870, 1871, and 1872, Under the Direction of the Secretary of the Smithsonian Institution*. Washington: U.S. Government Printing Office, 1875.

_____. "The Cañons of the Colorado." *Scribner's Monthly* 9 (January 1875): 392–310; (February, 1875): 394–409.

_____. "An Overland Trip to the Grand Cañon. *Scribner's Monthly* 10 (October 1875): 659–678.

"Raymond Jonson Is Interviewed." *El Palacio* 63 (May–June 1956): 144–45.

Robertson, Edna. *Gerald Cassidy, 1869–1934*. Santa Fe: Museum of New Mexico, 1977.

Ruffner, Budge. "Bruce A. Aiken." *Southwest Art* (November 1987): 39–44.

Ruland-Thorne, Kate. "Jerome Grimmer." *Southwest Art* (October 1988): 80–85.

Runte, Alfred. *Trains of Discovery: Western Railroads and the National Parks*. Niwot, Colorado: Roberts Rinehart, Inc., 1990.

Samuels, Harold, and Peggy Samuels. *Samuels' Encyclopedia of Artists of the American West*. 1976; revised edition, New York: Castle Books, 1985.

Sanders, Gordon E. *Oscar Berninghaus, Taos New Mexico: Master Painter of American Indians of the Frontier West* (Taos, New Mexico: Taos Heritage, 1985).

Schartz, Toby. "The Santa Fe Railway and Early Southwest Artists." *American West* (October 1982): 32–41.

Sherman, Lisa. "Woody Gwyn." *Artspace* 7 (Winter 1982–83): 39–42.

Simpson, William. "Thomas Moran—The Man." *Fine Arts Journal* 20 (January 1909): 24.

Skolnick, Arnold, and Suzan Campbell. *Paintings of the Southwest*. New York: Clarkson Potter, Inc., and Chameleon Books, 1994.

Standing Rainbows: Railroad Promotion of Art of the West and Its Native Peoples. Wichita: Kansas State of Historical Society, 1981.

Stanton, R. B. *Scribner's Monthly* articles, 1890.

Stanton, R. B. *Grand Canyon of Arizona*. Chicago: The Passenger Department of the Santa Fe Railway, 1909.

Stegner, Wallace. *Beyond the Hundredth Meridian: John Wesley Powell and the Second Opening of the West*. New York: Houghton Mifflin, 1953.

Stevens, Nina Spaulding. "Pilgrimage to the Artist's Paradise." *Fine Arts Journal* (February 11, 1911): 105–117.

Trenton, Patricia, ed. *Independent Spirits: Women Painters of the American West*. Berkeley: University of California Press, 1995.

Trenton, Patricia, and Peter Hassrick. *The Rocky Mountains: A Vision for Artists in the Nineteenth Century*. Norman: University of Oklahoma Press, 1983.

White, William Allen. *McClure's Magazine* (September 1905).

Woloshuk, Nicholas. *E. Irving Couse*. Santa Fe: Santa Fe Village Art Museum, 1976.

Woods, G. K., ed. *Personal Impressions of the Grand Cañon of the Colorado River Near Flagstaff, Arizona: As Seen Through Nearly Two Thousand Eyes, and Written in the Private Visitor's Book of the World-Famous Guide Capt. John Hance*. San Francisco: The Whitaker & Ray Co., 1899.

QUOTATIONS

Quotations that are not footnoted in the body of the text are credited here, listed by page number.

13: Joaquin Miller, *The Overland Monthly*, 1901.

14: Joseph Christmas Ives, *Report Upon the Colorado River of the West*, Senate Executive Document, 36th Congress. 1st Session, 1861.

15: Ibid.

16: John Wesley Powell, *Exploration of the Colorado River of the West and its Tributaries*, 1875, p. 194.

23: Fitz-James MacCarthy, "A Rhapsody," in *The Grand Canyon of Arizona* (Chicago: The Passenger Department of the Santa Fe Railway, 1906).

25: Wallace Stegner, *Beyond the Hundredth Meridian: The Exploration of the Grand Canyon and the Second Opening of the West*, 1953.

26: Ibid.

28: Charles Lummis, "The Greatest Thing in the World," in *The Grand Canyon of Arizona* (Chicago: The Passenger Department of the Santa Fe Railway, 1906).

30: George Warton James, *In and Around the Grand Canyon*, 1900, pp. 254–55.

37: J. Donald Hughes, *The Story of Man at the Grand Canyon* (Grand Canyon National Park, 1967).

38: Fitz-James MacCarthy, "A Rhapsody," in *The Grand Canyon of Arizona* (Chicago: Passenger Department of the Santa Fe, 1906).

40: Elliott Daingerfield, "Nature Versus Art," *Scribner's Monthly* 48 (February 1911): 255.

41: Harriet Monroe, in the *Chicago Record Herald*, quoted in *The Grand Canyon of Arizona* (Chicago: The Passenger Department of the Santa Fe Railway, 1906).

43: Elliott Daingerfield, writing of his own work in "Sketch of His Life," p. 2. Quoted in Estill Curtis Pennington and J. Richard Gruber, *Victorian Visionary: The Art of Elliott Daingerfield*, p. 41.

45: J. B. Priestly, *Midnight on the Desert*, 1937

48: William R. Leigh, in his journal, 1909.

50: Clarence Dutton, *Tertiary History of the Grand Cañon District*, 1882

53: John C. Van Dyke, *The Grand Canyon of the Colorado* (New York: Charles Scribner's Sons, 1920).

54: Edwin Corle, *Listen, Bright Angel* (New York: Edwin Corle, 1946), p. 226.

57: John Wesley Powell, "The Scientific Explorer," in *The Grand Canyon of Arizona* (Chicago: The Passenger Department of the Santa Fe Railway, 1906), p. 29.

60: Charles A. Brant, manager of the El Tovar Hotel at the Grand Canyon, in a letter to Carl Oscar Borg, 1916. Quoted in Helen Laird, *Carl Oscar Borg and the Magic Region*, 1986.

60: Carl Oscar Borg to his wife in 1937. Quoted in Helen Laird, *Carl Oscar Borg and the Magic Region*, 1986, p. 167.

61: Miner R. Tillotson and Frank J. Taylor, *Grand Canyon Country* (Stanford, California: Stanford University Press, 1929).

61: Poem by Carl Oscar Borg, n.d. Quoted in Helen Laird, *Carl Oscar Borg and the Magic Region*, 1986, p. 88.

63: Miner R. Tillotson and Frank J. Taylor, *Grand Canyon Country* (Stanford, California: Stanford University Press, 1929).

65: John Van Dyke, *The Grand Canyon of the Colorado: Recurrent Studies in Impressions and Appearances* (New York: Charles Scribner's Sons, 1920).

67: Richard Brewster Stanton, "Engineering in the Grand Canyon," in *The Grand Canyon of Arizona* (Chicago: The Passenger Department of the Santa Fe Railway, 1906), p. 49.

68: Clarence Dutton, *Tertiary History of the Grand Cañon District*, 1882

71: Mrs. Lillian B. Upson of Baldwinsville, New York, October, 30, 1892, in tour guide John Hance's guest book.

72: William Allen White, *McClure's Magazine* (September 1905).

78: Thomas D. Murphy, *Three Wonderlands of the American West* (Boston: L. C. Page & Co., 1913), p. 116.

80: Louis Akin in a letter to a friend regarding his 1905 exhibition. Cited in Bruce Babbitt, *Color and Light: The Southwest Canvases of Louis Akin*, pp. 17–18.

82: Emily Grant Hutchings, cited in Bill and Frances Spencer Belknap, *Gunnar Widforss: Painter of the Grand Canyon*, 1969, pp. 75–82.

86: George Wharton James, *In and Around the Grand Canyon* (Boston: Little, Brown, and Company, 1900), xv.

87: Thomas D. Murphy, *Three Wonderlands of the American West* (Boston: L. C. Page & Co., 1913), pp. 115–116.

90: Fitz-James MacCarthy, "A Rhapsody," in *The Grand Canyon of Arizona* (Chicago: The Passenger Department of the Santa Fe Railway, 1906), p. 95.

90: Arthur Wesley Dow, introduction to *The Color of the Grand Canyon of Arizona, Exhibition of Pictures by Arthur Wesley Dow*, Montross Gallery, New York, 1913.

91: Clarence Dutton, *Tertiary History of the Grand Cañon District*, 1882

94: Thomas Moran, "American Art and American Scenery," in Higgins, *The Grand Canyon* (Chicago: The Passenger Department of the Santa Fe Railway, 1897).

100: President Theodore Roosevelt in a speech at the Grand Canyon, 1903.

107: William J. Breed, "Our 'Unchanging' Canyon," *Arizona Highways* (May 1976).

108: Miner R. Tillotson and Frank J. Taylor, *Grand Canyon Country* (Stanford, California: Stanford University Press, 1929).

110: Painter William R. Leigh in his journal, 1909.

112: Joseph Wood Krutch, *Grand Canyon: Today and All Its Yesterdays* (New York: William Sloane Associates, 1958).

116: Colin Fletcher, *The Man Who Walked Through Time* (New York: Alfred Knopf, 1967).

119: John Van Dyke, *The Grand Canyon of the Colorado: Recurrent Studies in Impressions and Appearances* (New York: Charles Scribner's Sons, 1920).

123: J. B. Priestly, *Midnight on the Desert* (William Heinemann, Ltd., 1937).

124: Mrs. Mary E. Hart, M.D., of Los Angeles, June 5, 1895 in tour guide John Hance's guest book.

127: E. L. Kolb, *Through the Grand Canyon From Wyoming to Mexico* (New York: MacMillan Co., 1927).

132: Clarence Dutton, *Tertiary History of the Grand Cañon District*, 1882.

133: John Van Dyke, *The Grand Canyon of the Colorado: Recurrent Studies in Impressions and Appearances*. New York: Charles Scribner's Sons, 1920.

137: Herman D. Oleson, a visitor from Sweden, May 25, 1891 in tour guide John Hance's guest book.

140: Joseph Wood Krutch, *Grand Canyon: Today and All Its Yesterdays* (New York: William Sloane Associates, 1958).

143: Ibid.

147: C. A. Higgins, *The Grand Cañon of the Colorado River* (Chicago: The Passenger Department of the Santa Fe Railway and The Henry O. Shepherd Co., 1892, 1897).

149: Joseph Wood Krutch, Grand Canyon: *Today and All Its Yesterdays* (New York: William Sloane Associates, 1958).

150: John Colburn, "The Colorado Cañon," *The New York Times* (September 4, 1872).

153: John Van Dyke, *The Grand Canyon of the Colorado: Recurrent Studies in Impressions and Appearances* (New York: Charles Scribner's Sons, 1920).

156: President Theodore Roosevelt at the Grand Canyon, May 6, 1903.

156: William J. Breed, "Our 'Unchanging' Canyon," *Arizona Highways* (May 1976).

GEORGE HAWLEY HALLOWELL

GRAND CANYON, C. 1912

OIL ON CANVAS, 25 X 30 IN.

DEMARTINE-FREEDMAN COLLECTION

INDEX OF ARTISTS

Bruce Aiken 1, 105

Louis Akin 36–37, 76–77, 78–79, 80, 81, 82

Marion Boyd Allen 71

Vincent Archilesi 94, 101

Oscar Berninghaus 46, 50

Ernest L. Blumenschein 52

Carl Oscar Borg 39, 54, 60

Gustav Buek 30

Harry Paul Burlin 91

Earl Carpenter 4–5, 10, 122–123

Gerald Cassidy 57

John Cogan 126, 127

Samuel Colman 46–47

Howard Cook 74, 75

Eanger, Irving Couse 63

Dennis Culver 100

Elliott Daingerfield 40, 41, 43

Arthur Wesley Dow 90

F. W. von Egloffstein 14

Tony Foster 148–149

John Bond Francisco 64–65

Alyce Frank 153, 154–155

Mabel Frazer 68–69

Jerome Grimmer 116–117

Woody Gwyn 156

George Hawley Hallowell

Edith Hamlin 70

Peter Holbrook 124–125

William H. Holmes 24, 26–27

Clark Hulings 106–107

Wilson Hurley 132–133, 134–135, 136–137

Richard Iams 110, 111

Oscar B. Jacobson 61

Raymond Jonson 93

William Robinson Leigh 12–13, 48–49

Angus MacPherson 144

Merrill Mahaffey 102–103, 104–105

Frank Mason 108–109

Ed Mell 145, 146–147

Heinrich Balduin Möllhausen 15

Thomas Moran 20, 21, 22–23, 25, 32, 33, 34–35

Daniel Morper 118–119, 120–121

Peter A. Nisbet 138–139, 140–141, 142–143

Philip Pearlstein 97

William E. Porter 114–115

Edward Henry Potthast 44, 45, 51

Hanson Duvall Puthuff 53, 59

Warren E. Rollins 62

Louis Hovey Sharp 58

Susan Shatter 98, 150–151

George Gardner Symons 65, 66–67

Albert Tissandier 73

Walter Ufer 56

Curt Walters 2–3, 112–113

Mark Christopher Weber 128–129, 130–131

John Miller White 54–55

Gunnar M. Widforss 82–83, 84–85, 86, 87, 88, 89

Hiroshi Yoshida 72

Barbara Zaring 152–153, 154